Dudley Buck

Illustrations in Choir Accompaniment

With hints in registration. A hand-book (provided with marginal notes for

reference) for the use of organ students, organists, and those interested in church

music

Dudley Buck

Illustrations in Choir Accompaniment
With hints in registration. A hand-book (provided with marginal notes for reference) for the use of organ students, organists, and those interested in church music

ISBN/EAN: 9783337297305

Printed in Europe, USA, Canada, Australia, Japan

Cover: Foto ©Thomas Meinert / pixelio.de

More available books at **www.hansebooks.com**

ILLUSTRATIONS

IN

CHOIR ACCOMPANIMENT

WITH

HINTS IN REGISTRATION.

A HAND-BOOK

(PROVIDED WITH MARGINAL NOTES FOR REFERENCE)

FOR THE USE OF ORGAN STUDENTS, ORGANISTS, AND THOSE INTERESTED IN CHURCH MUSIC.

BY

DUDLEY BUCK.

NEW YORK:

G. SCHIRMER,

1880.

CONTENTS.

PRELIMINARY REMARKS.

TO learn how to be a good choir accompanist is by no means an elementary study. In fact, the pupil should possess a fair technical command of the instrument before making a special study of accompaniments. Given a reasonable degree of talent for acquiring execution, and nothing is more certain than that a good teacher will qualify such a pupil to play, satisfactorily, compositions written for the organ.

Technique necessary.

Mere organ studies, however, do not qualify a pupil as accompanist; for the organ student can, at least, give his undivided attention to the effects he is producing upon his instrument. The matter is rendered more complex when that instrument is to be properly handled *per se*, and at the same time properly subordinated to the various conditions of vocal accompaniment.

Organ studies proper, not sufficient.

Increasing power of execution does not, then, necessarily bring with it increasing ability to accompany well. This does not alter the fact that a good technical foundation is indispensable, for the natural gift in accompaniment can not develop without it. It simply argues a different and varied application of the technique acquired; which new application will be found to be deducible from the nature and requirements of the voices to be accompanied, rather than from the nature of the accompanying instrument.

Application of technique.

It is necessary then, at the very outset, for the student to have some idea as to what constitutes good accompaniment abstractly considered.

What constitutes good accompaniment.

It is difficult to define this, and yet even inexperienced singers instantly and instinctively realize whether they are well accompanied or not. If we analyze their feelings, we shall find that the sensation is twofold : that of *freedom* on the one hand, that of *support* upon the other; or the lack of both in case they are badly accompanied.

The sense of freedom on the part of individual singers arises from the fact, (1) that the accompanist does not hinder by his performance their own natural delivery of the piece as to manner or style, breathing, etc. ; and (2) does not overpower, or, in technical language, "cover" them.

Where the nature or difficulty of the passage to be executed requires the employment of greater power on the part of the accompanist (as in passages of difficult intonation, climax passages, and the like), that support is at once at hand in case of good accompaniment, as though singer and accompanist were guided by the same thought. This is the real secret which can not be taught—the actual anticipation, on the part of the accompanist, of what the singer desires and needs.

Usual course of study.

Students of the organ, while pursuing their studies, must necessarily confine themselves to organ-*playing*, not accompanying. Through pecuniary reasons, or otherwise, the pupil generally leaves the teacher before the subject of accompaniment is even theoretically touched upon. Nor is a teacher to be blamed for not expending time upon this subject when the pupil's technique is first to be assured to him.

The next step therefore is the assuming of an organ position. The young incumbent's stock in trade (so to speak) usually consists of a certain number of organ compositions, which he may play very well, and yet accompany the simplest tunes badly. The chances are that he has few, if any, theoretical views on the subject. His first steps, then, are made at hap-hazard, and, as experience shows, often result in deeply rooted faults, even where a great natural gift may exist.

Amateur organists.

Another class, by far more numerous, is that of the amateur, who is generally occupied in some mercantile (or at least not musical) capacity throughout the week, "presiding" at the organ on Sunday. Now, we have very many accomplished amateurs, but, taking the whole country into consideration, as a general thing the case is worse, for the technical foundation is, as a rule, quite deficient. The ambition of this class is ordinarily limited by the desire "to play *well enough to play in church*," quite innocent of the fact that to do this really *well* implies an ability reaching somewhat beyond the requirements of the service proper. The heart-rending treatment which the organ, as an accompanying instrument, not unfrequently receives at their hands is all too common. Yet when we consider the whole country, and the fact that comparatively few of this class have (outside the larger cities) any opportunity to listen to good models, the churches have cause to be grateful to them. In their case, the "spirit is indeed willing" if the technical ability is weak.

Purpose of this work.

To assist, as far as he may be able, those among both of these classes who would give this important subject the special attention it deserves—to point out at least the right direction—is the object which the author has proposed to himself in this work. He does not for a moment imagine that it can supply the place of good personal instruction, but simply hopes that it may be found useful in connection with such instruction, and also serve as a guide to those who can not command a competent teacher to direct their studies.

How to use this work.

About all that can be accomplished upon paper is to give a series of hints and suggestions, *which must be improved upon, added to, and infinitely varied* through gradually acquired practical experience and unremitting diligence on the part of the student, if a practical result is to be attained.

For convenience' sake, the subject under discussion is divided into separate heads, to each of which a chapter is devoted. The nature of the subject, however, is such that it is impossible to treat any one of these heads with any thing like completeness within the limits of the chapter specially assigned to it. The reason of this lies in the extremely close relationship which exists between some of these subdivisions, whereby much that is said of one will measurably apply to others. On this account, it will be well for the student to understand at the outset that, as he

Influence of successive chapters upon previous matter.

proceeds in the perusal of this work, he should strive to apply a new principle or idea which a new chapter may contain to the completion of a principle advanced in some former chapter. Thus, while clearness of comprehension is promoted by these subdivisions, it must be the student's aim to make one section complete the other, and thus, at least measurably, obviate the author's shortcomings. To aid in this, frequent references to other chapters have been introduced.

The author has endeavored in all cases where he has advocated the use, or counselled the avoidance, of a given manner of accompaniment or registration, not to make it the simple assertion of an opinion, but to give the "*reason why.*" He believes it to be the only way by which the student can deduce truly general principles, and thus make the work available to his own requirements.

It will be noticed that nothing is said concerning the accompaniment of anthems. It was deemed unnecessary to make such a special heading, as the accompaniment of a somewhat elaborate anthem may bring into play the principles advanced in the majority of all the chapters given. If the various forms of accompaniment are well understood, their possible union in one and the same piece will not be found difficult.

Of Anthems.

In the examples and illustrations that follow, a medium-sized organ is assumed, as being generally within the reach of those using this work, and in most cases one of two manuals.

Preliminary requirements.

It is further assumed that those making use of this work are familiar with the elements of Harmony, at least to the extent of a knowledge of intervals, the ordinary progressions of chords, etc.

CHAPTER I.

GENERAL PRINCIPLES OF REGISTRATION AS APPLIED TO ACCOMPANIMENT.

For what class this chapter is intended.

A FAIR knowledge of registration, or the appropriate use and combination of stops, properly belongs to the acquirements assumed to be already possessed by students desirous of giving especial attention to the subject of accompaniments. It is of the first importance, however, to take as little for granted as possible in a work of this kind. To the experienced accompanist, and measurably to those of less experience but of great natural gifts, it not unfrequently seems strange, on the one hand, that others should not accompany properly; on the other hand, it seems to them as if they had *always known* the essential principles which they now practice. For such as these this book is not intended, much less this chapter, but for the great majority who are uncertain how to proceed and desirous of a guide in the right direction.

Our present standpoint.

Besides this, our present point of view differs somewhat from that of the various organ schools. The problem is not merely that of ascertaining the effect of a stop or combination of stops, considered as an *organ effect*, but as to its use or value as a *means of accompanying the voice*. We therefore propose to devote our opening chapter to the general consideration of this subject. The subsequent chapters, dealing with particular forms of accompaniment, will doubtless contain more or less repetition of ideas here presented. Reiteration, in a matter as complex as this, can, however, only result in fixing the attention upon the points at issue.

In what sense Registration may be taught.

It is the author's conviction that registration, in any complete or elaborate sense, can not be taught, but that it may be learned. If this seem paradoxical, a simile drawn from the practice of a sister art—Painting—may serve to make this clear.

A comparative beginner in this latter art, whose master instructs him how to apply certain colors to a given painting, could doubtless reproduce his work were the same subject given him and the same colors and shades of color supplied him. Under changed conditions, he would be helpless. What then is the course pursued? The student must learn to mix colors, and produce his own shades through experimental knowledge of the general principles which govern the process. These general principles will still apply to the changed conditions he is sure to meet with in his own work. They afford him a sure criterion of judgment as to how to proceed when removed from his master's advice and counsel, and implant within him that germ which it is his own responsibility to develop.

Marking Registration for given Pieces.

Thus with the organ. A master may carefully mark given pieces as to the use of certain stops. The student takes it to another instrument, and the effect is found to be quite different, and in most cases unsatisfactory. The tone-color does not suit the new conditions. With the painter it is not the mere knowledge how to manipulate the brush, nor with the organist how to manipulate the keys, but behind that must lie a knowledge of general principles of combination which can be adapted to varying circumstances. The student of accompaniments has, moreover, the double difficulty to contend with, that different voices (individuals) and classes of voice (male or female) require different modes and degrees of support, in addition to the constant differences among the instruments themselves.

These *general* principles, then, can be *taught*—their infinite modifications, through which alone they are made to apply to particular cases, must, after all, be *learned*, and that through experience and experiment after the pupil has left the master. That "whatever sounds well is correct" may be essentially true, but it is manifestly a poor rule to follow. For that which sounds badly to the trained and cultivated ear is not unfrequently listened to with complacency by the uncultivated. This is proved, in turn, by the wretched combinations we are sometimes called upon to endure in our churches—combinations inconsistent with the very nature of the instrument, as well as with place and occasion. Neither is this confined exclusively to small towns and out-of-the-way places ! *General principles only are useful.*

The organ manual-compass usually extends from CC to a^2 (thrice marked a^*)—namely, *Of Compass.*

The older instruments only to f^3—some of the modern ones extend the compass also to c^4.

This compass is seen to be much less than that of the pianoforte. On the other hand, the organ possesses manual stops which *sound* one and two octaves higher as compared with the vocal notation; also those which give the lower octave. This, taken in connection with the pedal organ (which in the largest instruments contains stops which produce the second octave lower), gives to the organ a compass (that is, to the ear, irrespective of the *number of keys*) actually much greater than that of the pianoforte.

It is evident that for purposes of accompaniment, we must, first of all, employ stops which are in unison with the voice as to pitch, as well as agreeing in quality. Such stops are those of eight feet. *Stops of eight feet.*

By this expression is meant a stop whose lowest tone is produced by a pipe eight feet long.

As the scale ascends, the length of the pipes decreases, the length being reduced one half for each octave.† Thus the tone in a stop whose initial tone is CC (actual pitch) is given by a pipe of four feet length. is given by one of two feet, and by one of one foot. From this point the reduction goes on to the extreme limit in fractions of a foot, a matter which concerns the organ-builder, but not the player.

It will be seen from the above that a four-foot stop will necessarily form the octave to the eight-foot; a two-foot will give the octave to the four-foot, or super-octave, etc. Thus, with a four-foot stop, if the key represented by be touched, the tone heard will be

---

* For a full explanation of this manner of indicating pitch, see the excellent work entitled, "A Primer of Modern Tonality," by John H. Cornell, page 12. G. Schirmer, New York.

† Organ-builders distinguish between *actual* and "speaking length"—that is, pipes which, for instance, appear in front of an organ, and serve for ornament as well as use, are often of greater length than the tone requires. This is adjusted by "cutting-down" in the rear of the pipe (out of sight) until the true ("speaking") length or pitch is attained. This of metal pipes only.

as compared with vocal notation. The same key touched with a two-foot stop drawn will give etc., etc. In the mean time the manual sixteen-foot stop gives the octave lower than written. It is well for the pupil to realize the actual effect of a simple chord played upon

Stops of sixteen, four and two feet.

the manual only with sixteen- eight- four- and two-foot stops drawn. The following (*a*) shows the keys touched, and (*b*) the tones which result from this chord.

The notes here placed side by side show the "doublings" produced by the various stops. The student should carefully examine so as to see which stop produces them. It will be remembered that this is simply a manual-chord without pedal-bass. This gives some conception of the reason for the power and majesty of the organ.

Fundamental principle of Registration.

From the preceding we deduce as a *fundamental principle*, both in accompaniment and in the use of the organ as a solo-instrument, *the predominance of the eight-foot-tone as being in unison with the voice*. The violation of this principle more frequently leads to bad combinations in accompaniment than the selection of unsuitable *qualities* of tone for a given piece. The stops of high pitch are comparatively valueless in accompaniment unless they rest upon the eight-foot tone as a foundation. They then add brilliancy to the effect, and become indispensable for such purpose.

When four-foot tone may be added.

To know when it is proper to add four-foot stops to an eight-foot accompaniment, it is simply necessary for the student to realize the following conditions:

1. Whether the eight-foot tone is so firmly established as to warrant this addition. The expression, eight-foot tone, is here to be understood as applied to the voices as well as to the accompaniment itself. If the voices are powerful enough to firmly establish this, the effect of the octaves added by means of the four-foot stops will always be good; especially if the character of the piece is of a cheerful nature. For brilliant effects, with a chorus of sufficient power, stops of two feet become necessary. These are the Fifteenth,* or Super-octave, the Piccolo, etc.

Characteristics of low and high tones.

2. Sounds of low pitch have the greatest "travelling quality" so-called. Thus the pedal tones of the organ or the double-basses (*contrabassi*) of an orchestra may be plainly distinguished *outside* the building within which the sound is produced, when the ear can not detect either melody or harmony. At a reasonable distance from the production of the tone—as within the audience-room — the stops or instruments of high pitch assert themselves in the most unmistakable manner. They can not be covered by those of lower pitch. It is this characteristic which should constantly be remembered in accompaniment, for if the preponderance of the four-foot tone be too great in proportion to the voices, they cease to blend together. It is this reason which causes organ-builders to place fewer stops of high pitch, and still fewer of low (sixteen-foot) tone, in their instruments as compared with the standard eight-foot tone.

Balance, as regards the voices.

Notwithstanding this fact, it still remains for the student to adapt the proportions to the voices he has to accompany; for though the balance of the instrument may be correct within itself, the balance as regards the voices will constantly vary. In the accompaniment of solos, duets, quartets, etc., especial care should be exercised as to the introduction of four-foot stops,

---

* Fifteenth—so called because the octave being represented by the eighth degree above a given tone, the following octave (ascending) falls upon the fifteenth degree. Thus the name represents the pitch of the stop in relation to the unison-tone.

for here the *preponderance** of the upper octave can easily show itself, unbalancing the proper effect. When the voices to be accompanied are more numerous, this can not so readily occur. Much will depend upon the voicing of the stops in question as to their use or omission.

When voices are sufficiently powerful to easily sustain four-foot tone, in fact to require it, the addition of sixteen-foot tone to the manuals becomes desirable. This addition is specially useful when dignity and solidity of tone are required. As the tone of the sixteen-foot stops lies *below* the voice, their use can not so easily be abused as in case of a preponderance of four-foot tone ; as the latter will then cease to assimilate with the voice. Used without the four-foot stops, however, the sixteen-foot manual-tone would frequently have a tendency to obscure the harmony, through the too prominent assertion of the lower octave. When the four-foot stops are added to those of sixteen and eight feet, the eight-foot standard tone retains, so to speak, its equilibrium, by means of the opposite relations of pitch created, on the one hand, by the four-foot stops, and by those of sixteen feet upon the other. *(margin: Sixteen-foot tone; when to be added.)*

The use of Mixtures or Compound Stops (which give several tones to each key struck) is only justifiable in accompanying a very powerful choir, large chorus, or a whole congregation. A possible exception to this may be the use of the Swell Mixture, when the Full Swell is drawn as accompaniment to comparatively few voices. This on account of its relatively mild effect. Even in this case, it should not be long continued. *(margin: Mixtures.)*

Although it does not lie within the scope of this work to enter into any exhaustive treatment of the *nature* of the stops, yet it may here be said that nothing will aid the acquirement of a good registration more surely than a knowledge of the stops from this point of view. The student should inform himself as to their various shapes, lengths, whether of metal, wood, or both, and, their characteristics being familiar, their use will far more readily be acquired.† As to the Mixtures, it is absolutely necessary to have such knowledge of their nature as to comprehend the reason why they may be used with many voices, but not with few. This reason is entirely apart from their relative *power*, as will be seen. The Mixtures produce what would ordinarily be understood as discords. If the pupil would realize this, let him draw the Great

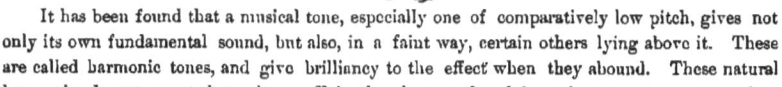

Organ Dulciana, holding this chord : To this add the Twelfth, and the following tones are heard in addition : Two of the tones thus heard—namely, *B* and *D*, are seen to be foreign to the chord held on the manual. The Twelfth and Fifteenth together would constitute a simple Mixture of two ranks of pipes. Other Mixtures would also give to the above fundamental chord the tones : so that with certain stops drawn, the following conglomeration of tones is actually produced :

It has been found that a musical tone, especially one of comparatively low pitch, gives not only its own fundamental sound, but also, in a faint way, certain others lying above it. These are called harmonic tones, and give brilliancy to the effect when they abound. These natural harmonics do not assert themselves sufficiently when produced by unison or octave organ-pipes *(margin: Harmonic tones.)*

---

* It is to be understood that it is not the *perception* of the four-foot tone by the ear which constitutes a bad effect, often quite the contrary, but a *preponderance* of the same.

† The best work for this purpose is that entitled, "The Organ and its Construction," by Ed. J. Hopkins. London : Robert Cocks & Co.

(they are best heard in stringed instruments); therefore organ-builders supply this lack by adding certain ranks of pipes to sound the tones required. Thus, with Mixtures of four or five " ranks," so-called, we have four or five distinct tones respectively on touching *one key* of the manual.

It is evident that if these foreign tones should be distinctly heard, the effect would be *Felt, rather than heard.* detestable, but they are so modified by proper voicing* that when all the sixteen- eight- and four-foot stops are drawn they may be said to be *felt*, in added brilliancy and solidity, rather than *actually heard* as to the intervals in question. It was this fact which led Berlioz (whose knowledge of this particular subject was limited), in his famous treatise on " Modern In-strumentation," to remark that " it remains to be explained how that *which is not heard* can produce a good effect." This is witty, but the fact remains; as the student can readily ascertain at the instrument by comparing the registration—" Full with and without Mixtures." All the instruction necessary to fully elucidate this point (which is altogether beyond the scope of this chapter) may be found in Hopkins' large and admirable work, Chap. XXIV., page 147. (See second note, bottom of page 7.)

For our present purpose, it is sufficient to call attention to the fact that the characteristics above mentioned forbid the use of Mixtures with voices, except where great power and brilliancy are required, and where the number of the voices precludes the possibility of the unison (eight-foot) tone being obscured in any sense. They require all the foundation and octave stops to have been already drawn. If otherwise used, Mixtures annihilate all vocal effects.

Tone qualities. In our modern instruments, we now find four qualities of tone—namely, Diapason, Flute, Reed, and String tone. This latter, as of comparatively recent introduction in this country, is usually lacking in the older instruments.

Diapasons. The Open Diapason has, or should have, that broad and resonant quality which makes it truly the foundation of the organ. Its quality is sometimes, and with justice, described as " organ-tone," not merely on account of its giving this foundation, but also because it resembles nothing else. No other instrument has this quality. The other classes of stops mentioned, as their names indicate, bear more or less resemblance to the orchestral wind instruments, except the string-toned stops, which only under certain conditions resemble the stringed instruments of the orchestra.

The term " open" as applied to the Diapason denotes literally that it is composed of open pipes—that is, without a stopper or plug at one end, as in case of the Stopped Diapason. Its name, however, *does not* denote one fact—namely, that it is always made of metal (the Diapason of six-teen feet in the Pedal Organ excepted), while the Stopped Diapason is usually made of wood.

In its relations to the voice, the Open Diapason is the most valuable of all stops. This is on account of its full tone as a means of support, and especially on account of what may be termed its " *neutral tint* " as to quality—agreeing, as it does, with voices of all kinds, and entering readily into combination with all other organ-stops.

Principal; Fifteenth. The Octave and Super-octave to the eight-foot Diapason are respectively the Principal and the Fifteenth. These have the same *quality* of tone, but are far more self-asserting as respects use with voices than the Open Diapason, on account of their higher pitch. For this reason, it may happen that when the vocal power is sufficient to warrant a slight degree of increased brilliancy in the accompaniment—in other words, an addition of four-foot tone—the addition of the

---

* Especially where duplications and reduplications of the fundamental occur, *that* tone is strengthened in the Mixture against a weaker power in the other intervals given.

Principal or Octave may be found somewhat too radical. As a compromise to this, we have Flutes of four feet which admirably answer this purpose and give a more delicate octave.

We have used the terms Principal or Octave as synonyms for the same metal stop of four feet. The name " Principal" has come into general use in England and America, as indicating this particular four-foot stop, in the following way: In tuning the organ, " the temperament is first set" in this stop—that is, it is itself first tuned as perfectly as possible. *To it*, as a standard, are subsequently tuned all the remaining stops; those of the Pedal Organ included. The selection of this stop arises from its standing, as it were, midway in pitch between the extreme high and extreme low compass of the instrument, and possessing throughout its range the firm diapason quality. It is evident, then, that it is, in a sense, *the principal stop to the organ-builder.* The selection and use of this name are, however, to be regretted, for the names of stops should have a special significance *to the player*, to whom it is *not the principal* stop. Similarly, the word *Diapason* is derived from two Greek words signifying literally " through all"—that is, the scale. In organs where the compass of *each* stop " goes through" the scale, this name has manifestly no significance as applied to the stop in question. Neither does it give any idea of the relation of the stop to the instrument as a whole. The Germans have a far better system, as it is logical. Thus they name our Open Diapason the *Principal* of sixteen or eight feet, as the case may be. It *is* the principal stop. The English " Principal " then becomes the " Octave," etc.

Derivation of the words " Principal" and " Diapason."

The Flutes of an organ constitute one of the most valuable subdivisions of the instrument as a means of accompaniment. Of less power than the Diapasons, the mellow and pervading tone of the eight-foot Flutes adapts itself admirably to accompaniments where the more incisive quality of the Diapasons would be too positive, while the four-foot Flutes add a clear brilliancy often better suited to the voice than the more positive Principal of four feet. To give such an accompaniment a slight shade of the " metal tone," together with a slight increase of power, the Dulciana of the Great or Choir Organ is frequently added to the eight-foot Flutes. This still leaves the flute quality predominating, but shades it with a slightly sombre tint which harmonizes well with the voice. Such characteristic effects, especially when the change intended is but slight, are of vastly more significance in our organs of comparatively recent construction and improved voicing than is the case with the older instruments. These latter, while often possessing many stops of sweet quality, are generally very deficient in contrasts of tone, so that such an addition as the above would scarcely be perceived. For this reason, more stops have usually to be drawn in case of an old instrument than with a modern one. This more particularly affects solo-accompaniment, and is unfortunate, for the assemblage of an increased number of poorly-voiced, uncharacteristic stops, although somewhat increasing the power, does not improve the quality, but has quite the contrary effect.

Flutes.

Slight changes of Registration in our older Organs.

A special use of the eight-foot Flutes may here be noted as used in combination with the Open Diapason of eight feet, or with string-toned stops, and especially valuable in accompaniment.

Flutes combined with Diapasons.

The addition of an eight-foot Flute to an eight-foot Diapason does not seem to materially change the *power*, but it materially changes the *quality*. The Diapason still asserts its superior strength, but the tone of the Flute seems to envelop and soften it; and, while it thus deprives the former stop of a portion of its incisive character, it gives it—as has sometimes been said—a " velvety quality." Thus, in such pieces as require a full, mellow, but not powerful accompaniment, the eight-foot Flute serves to mediate between the positive tone of the Open Diapason and the voices. This characteristic is observed in a still more marked degree when the Flute enters into combination with string-tones (of which later).

Stopped Diapasons. The Flutes we have had in mind in the above remarks were "open" Flutes. The Stopped Diapasons, however, whether of wood or metal, deserve to be classified here from the player's standpoint, on account of their essentially flute-like quality, especially in modern instruments. Compared with the "open" Flutes, they differ to such an extent that they afford the organist opportunity for pleasant contrasts of tone within the flute quality itself.

Reeds. The Reed-stops differ from all others in that their tone is not produced by the resonance of a pipe, but by the vibration of a small tongue of metal. In our medium-sized two-manual Organs they generally comprise in the Great Organ the Trumpet of eight feet, and occasionally the Clarionet in addition. In such case, the compass of the latter stop rarely goes below four-foot C.

In the Swell Organ we find the Oboe (or Hautboy) and the Trumpet (or Cornopean); the latter name being given when of large scale and powerful intonation. If the Organ has three manuals, we find the Clarionet placed upon the Choir Organ.

Tuning. All of these stops, while of the most decided and agreeable character if well made, are, by the very nature of their construction, very sensitive to change of temperature. Hence they are the first to get out of tune in any organ. Their value is so great in producing variety in accompaniment, that all organists in our smaller cities and towns where there is no organ-builder resident, or where a professional tuner's visits are few and far between, should learn to *tune* and *clean* the reeds themselves. This is very easily acquired by asking for such instruction whenever an experienced tuner chances to be present, who will doubtless willingly give the desired information. This will give the organist constant use of these stops if he so desires, whereas it otherwise often happens that they remain unavailable for a long period, or are used in a condition which makes their effect intolerable to a sensitive ear. In many places, more especially in our smaller towns, we find lady-organists. To them the above advice does not apply. A lady's dress is, unfortunately, an insuperable barrier to tuning, as it would imperil too many pipes in arriving at those to be tuned.

Use of Reeds in harmonic accompaniment (Simple Chords). The eight-foot reeds of the Swell will rarely be found available for an accompaniment in full chords at a less degree of power than *mezzo-forte;* the four-foot reeds of the Swell scarcely ever, except when the Full Swell is employed; the four-foot reed of the Great Organ never, except when the Full Organ (or at least Full without Mixtures) becomes necessary. The extremely pungent character of modern reeds renders a careful use of them necessary, and they should not be used long continuously, but rather to heighten the effect of given passages. They are eminently useful for solo effects (of the organ), but when used in the accompaniment of solos, more especially of the female voice, they require particular treatment. This will be discussed under the head of "Obligato Accompaniment." It is usual to add a Stopped Diapason to the reed to give it more "body" or fullness. This is specially advisable when employed in accompaniment. It is not to be denied, however, that, in case of many finely-voiced modern reeds, used in *obligato* accompaniment, the reed alone will produce the most characteristic effect. We have reeds of sixteen, eight, and four feet in our largest church-organs, and they are even made of thirty-two-foot tone.*

---

* We have, at present, but one specimen of a thirty-two-foot reed in a church-organ in the United States, so far as the author is aware—namely, in the Jesuit Church of Chicago.

In addition to the stops of this class previously mentioned, we find the following in the larger instruments: In the Great Organ—the Trumpet of sixteen feet and the Clarion of four feet. In the Swell—the Vox Humana of eight feet, the Double Trumpet or Contra-Fagotto of sixteen feet, and Clarion of four feet. In the Pedal Organ—the Trombone of sixteen feet and the Trumpet of eight feet. *[margin: Additional Reeds in large Organs.]*

Besides these, we occasionally find (in the Swell or Choir Organ) the Euphone of sixteen feet or Cor Anglais (English Horn) of eight feet. The first of these gives, in its Tenor range, a very beautiful imitation of the orchestral Bassoon. These are so-called " free" reeds, an explanation of which (in contradistinction to the other so-called " striking reeds") can not be entered into here. (See Hopkins' work, previously referred to.) A " Cabinet Organ" reed would be a familiar specimen of the " free" species. The two stops above named are unfit for purposes of accompaniment, except, and that rarely, in its obligato form. The Oboe (Hautboy) of the swell is sometimes divided into two registers, called respectively Oboe (or Oboe Treble) and Bassoon Bass. In such case they form but one stop of complete compass when drawn together, the name being derived from the fact that the orchestral Bassoon is the natural bass of the orchestral Oboe.

The string-toned stops comprise the Gamba, eight feet (Great Organ); the Salicional, eight feet (Swell Organ); the Violin, Violina, or Fugara, four feet (Swell or Choir Organ); the Geigenprincipal (Violin Diapason), of eight feet; the Keraulophon, eight feet (Choir Organ); the Violone, sixteen feet, and Violoncello, eight feet (Pedal Organ). The former stop* is usually made of wood, but when made of metal it is frequently called the *Contrebasse* or Contra-Gamba. These stops differ in degree of " stringiness," the Gamba having the most characteristic quality in this respect as a rule. Lastly, the Dulciana (Great or Choir) may, from the *organist's standpoint*, sometimes be included in this list. Strictly speaking, it does not belong to the stringtones. It may, however, be considered as the connecting link in quality between the stringtones proper and the Diapasons. Where an organ is of sufficient size to possess several string-toned stops, the Dulciana is usually voiced with less of that quality. In small two-manual instruments which possess no string-tone on the Great Organ (although they may have one on the Swell), our modern builders frequently give the Dulciana a somewhat decided string quality. *[margin: String-tones.]* *[margin: The Dulciana as related to String-tones and Diapasons.]*

Less radical than the reeds, but still of very marked quality, the string-toned stops are extremely valuable for purposes of accompaniment. They do not " pervade" nor " carry" tone to a distance like an Open Diapason, but without this power they are nevertheless quickly *felt* by voices, their crisp quality apparently giving a very distinct sense of the accompanying harmonies. *[margin: General characteristics of the "String-tones."]*

Their characteristic string quality, as resembling the stringed instruments of the orchestra, is best heard in comparatively slow, and especially in chromatic progressions. In fact, the speech of these stops is essentially slow. Trills are always to be avoided, except with several assisting stops and some of higher pitch. Their voicing and quickness of speech have been much improved of late years, but the above still holds good. On this account, they are usually employed in combination with Stopped Diapasons or Flutes of eight feet, which " help them to their speech," as it is termed, and also serve to unite their quality with that of the voices to be accompanied, as with the reeds.

The four-foot string-tone, usually placed only in the Swell in organs of moderate dimensions (Violin or Violina), is rarely satisfactory in accompaniment, except where the Full Swell may be employed. The upper octave of string quality (above the voices) which this stop gives, although very effective in organ solo combinations, does not readily harmonize with solo voices or the *[margin: Four-foot String-tone.]*

---

* The *Violone* is spoken of.

accompaniment of a quartet. At a short distance from the performer, its tone seems to be heard side by side with the vocal effect, but not *blending* with it.

Contrast; application of principles. If it be desired to contrast one quality of tone with another, the pupil may feel safe in making any combination whatever to this end, if he will but bear in mind the fundamental rule respecting *predominance* of the eight-foot tone. Perhaps the most striking contrast the organ possesses is that of reed tone upon one manual and flute tone upon another. This *generally* proves most effective when the reed lies lower than the flute-part, or, in other words, when the reed is assigned to the left and the flute quality to the right hand. A simple inversion of this will produce a combination of quite different effect. String and flute tone also contrast excellently in this manner. It is only in accompaniments of a certain kind—those in which the accompaniment contains a melodic significance of its own, independent of the voices—that such tone contrasts are particularly available or even desirable.

The Quintadena. A very beautiful stop of eight feet, introduced in the Swell Organ by some of our builders, is the *Quintadena*. It is somewhat string-like in quality, and, as its name implies, gives a fifth or "quint" as a quite perceptible harmonic in connection with any given tone of its scale. This compound effect is produced from one pipe, and not from separate ones, as in case of the Mixtures. On account of the strong harmonic referred to, the Quintadena is unsuited to accompaniment, unless well covered by an independently balanced combination. Used in this manner, it may be employed to "brighten" an accompaniment.

Very beautiful solo effects may be obtained from it in conjunction with a Flute, four feet, and Tremulant *ad libitum*.

It rests with the student to make himself familiar through actual experiment with the various shades of tone color referred to. He will find them differing in degree in every instrument, but, however varied their quality or pitch, they must all be subordinated to the one simple law of eight feet or unison predominance—by closely observing which, he can not go astray, and experience will teach him the possible exceptions.

In most of our modern instruments the length (eight feet, etc.) is marked upon each stop. Besides this, the student should learn to distinguish them instantly by ear.

CHAPTER II.

ACCOMPANIMENT OF THE CHORALE, OR PLAIN "HYMN-TUNE."*

EXAMPLE 1 (AS WRITTEN AND SUNG).

EXAMPLE 2 (AS PLAYED).

---

* We purposely use the word "hymn-tune"—"hymnody," etc.—in this work, as the "psalm-tune" would, logically speaking, be a chant. The psalm is, in the absence of metre, essentially a prose composition, and we either chant prose or set it in anthem form. The hymn—even if derived from the psalms—is a metrical composition in the strict sense.

Syllabic repetition. THE preceding familiar tune has been selected as a specimen of certain *syllabic repetitions of the same chord.* (See measures 4–5 and others.) The idea has prevailed in many quarters that such repetitions in the voices should not be repeated upon the Organ, but held out a time equal to the value of the notes were they tied together. This is very objectionable when the voices are silent, as all rhythmic flow is thereby destroyed. In accompanying the voices, this may be less objectionable, but had better be avoided as disturbing the rhythmic relation between player and singers.

True manner of performance. The true manner of performing such passages is by a compromise, as given in No. 2—*e* and *e.* The Bass and Alto, by sustaining *F* in octaves, so bind the passage together that the strict *legato* effect is preserved, while the repetition of Soprano and Tenor notes keeps the rhythm intact. Attention is also called to the fact that the motion occurs in one outer part (Soprano), and one inner (Tenor), while the sustained tones bear the same relation. (See Alto and Bass.) This combination of motion and repose gives both smoothness and distinctness as results.

Doubling the Manual Bass. Example 2, *a.* Omitting the pedal part throughout, and playing the tune through once upon the Swell Organ, would constitute the simplest form of "giving out the tune" so-called. Should this be adopted, it will be noticed that the latter half of the tune is essentially the repetition of the first eight measures. A change of effect for this latter half can here be produced (without affecting the simplicity) by doubling the bass, or playing it in the lower octave, the right hand carrying out the three-part harmony, thus:

EXAMPLE 3.

(measure 9.)

While thus played through, the Great and Pedal Organs are supposed to be already prepared. The following (Example 4) shows the ending as first played through upon the Swell, and the beginning of the voices (chorus or congregation) accompanied on the Great Organ.

EXAMPLE 4.

Manual.

Gr.

N.B.—Gr. to Ped.

Pedal.

Beginning the tune after "giving it out." At N. B. it is to be noted that the Great to Pedal Coupler is drawn simultaneously with the *second* half note. In this way the sixteen-foot tone of the Pedals is heard upon the first part of the measure, and the loud eight and four feet of the Great Manual on drawing the coupler with the latter half of the measure. This not only serves to mitigate the abruptness of the change from the Swell to the powerfully registered Great Organ, but it also serves as a sort of signal, enabling choir and

congregation to begin more promptly together. This occurs during the time allowed for the
⌢ (last note of previous examples—compare with No. 4 at *.)

The exact reverse of the manner of beginning the tune advocated in Example 4 is some- Another
times heard after the tune has been played over once upon the Swell. Example 5 illustrates this. manner. Ob-
jections to the

EXAMPLE 5.

Here it is seen that instead of the Pedal entering same.
upon the first half of the second measure, the Great
Organ enters abruptly upon the second half of the
measure with the upper note of the harmony alone.
This is very objectionable except in the rarest cases,
but it is far too frequently heard in our churches. It
is illogical, in that the foundation should come first
and not the superstructure. The chord should be
built up from its fundamental tone to be agree-
able to the ear. As it is, it sounds like a continual advertisement of the fact that the accompanist
expects the choir's intonation to be faulty, and that, *before they begin to sing*, they must be
assisted. In such large Episcopal churches as have a double choir, one on each side of the
chancel, an exception in this regard may perhaps be excusable at times: especially in responsive and unisonous chanting. This is more particularly for the benefit of the choir farthest
removed from the organ or accompanist. The constant recurrence of this mode of commencement
in successive verses of a hymn is extremely unmusical, and had better be entirely avoided.

We will now suppose the tune to proceed as in Example 2, the Pedals being employed Use of Pedal-
throughout. It will be noticed that they are here played an octave lower than the vocal bass stops in the
lower octave.
notation. The sixteen-foot pedal-stops, speaking an octave lower than written, thus sound two
octaves distant from the vocal bass. The eight-foot stops of the Pedal and those of the Manuals
(coupled to the Pedal) give the single octave lower than the vocal bass, while the fingers on the
Manuals give the actual unison with that part. It is this treatment of the Pedals which, in tunes
of this class, gives a strong and solid foundation suitable to the support of a large chorus. This
also justifies the employment of stops of high pitch, Mixtures, etc. In tunes of another class, it
will be found that another principle obtains, which will be considered elsewhere.

Example 2—*a, c, e.* The notes here repeated are *not to be struck staccato.* The finger Touch.
should not leave the key, but the key should be allowed to come up with such promptness as to
ensure the quick closing of the wind-chest valve (*pallet*), thus cutting off the tone, which is
instantly resumed by the succeeding fall of the finger. This requires some practice to ensure
distinctness and smoothness combined.

Example 2—*b, d, f.* Supplementary harmonies are here added, as will be seen by Supplement-
comparison with Example 1. This is not obligatory, but when judiciously and naturally ary Harmo-
nies.
employed is effective. Care must be taken not to make such additions when the compass runs
low, as they then have a tendency to obscure the harmonic progressions.

The apparent consecutive octaves in the bass (last measure but one) are here unobjectionable Consecutive
because the four-part harmony is complete and correct, and the effect is simply Octaves.
that of strengthening the bass. Here, too, the Pedal ceases to be played in
the lower octave, and springs a sixth, thus :   This is necessitated by Pedal
changes.
the Pedal compass not possessing the low B flat, but the pupil should note that afterward it

does not return thus : [♭] This is on account of a better (more natural) harmonic
progression. Care should be exercised, where such alterations are necessary, to make them in
such a manner as may least violate the natural flow of the bass, considered melodically by itself.

Two more specimens of this kind of treatment follow. The pupil should carefully compare
them with the vocal score, which may be found in almost any collection of tunes.

EXAMPLE 6.

At *a* and *c* the rhythmic repetition ceases in the Soprano, *as the other parts have sufficient
motion of their own to preserve the rhythm intact.* At *b* and *d* supplementary harmonies,
already spoken of, are introduced. At *e* the passing of the sustained tone from the thumb of the
right to that of the left hand is to be noted. This renders the execution of the following
measure easy, which would otherwise require the following displacement of the hand.
The employment of similar substitution of one hand for the other will be
found useful in very many tunes.

EXAMPLE 7.

Pedals in the
upper octave.   The Pedals should be used throughout in accompanying these tunes, not necessarily in
"giving them out," and both feet should be employed, without which no strict legato can be
preserved. In this last example, it is perhaps better not to play the Pedals an octave lower than
written. This is partly on account of the limited upward compass (for it will be remembered
that the higher the compass the greater the necessity for a deep and solid foundation in choral
tunes), and partly depends upon the size and quality of the Organ. In all cases where the Pedals
are played *as written*, the left hand must omit the Bass, playing only the Tenor. This forms
one of the simplest introductions to obligato pedal-playing, and can not be too strongly recom-

mended as a habit. Experience, and a good ear, can alone determine whether the Pedals should be used in this manner or in the lower octave. When the chorus is very powerful, the lower octave is preferable. When it is only of medium power, the obligato form is better. As an organ effect, considered by itself, the obligato form is nearly always preferable.

At *b* it will be noticed that the Soprano *G* is held throughout the measure, while the other

parts cease thus:  This exceptional effect will sometimes be found of use when Sustained upper tone; (Soprano.)

choir or congregation become unsteady either in time or tune. This is more likely to occur in tunes of higher compass than this; but the principle holds good, and can be introduced occasionally at other points than the middle of the tune, but not at the beginning of the same. (See remarks following Example 5.) The single tone in this illustration is heard only as the singers pause for breath, and the resumption of the chord in the following measure acts as a powerful accentuation, especially through the re-entrance of the Pedals, steadying the voices in both respects above noted.

At *c*, attention is called to a means of producing an absolute legato effect frequently Of the strict legato. resorted to in accompanying slow movements upon the organ. The passage written in the voice

parts as [music] is played as if written thus: [music] the motion

passing from above to below the Alto note (*E*) which remains stationary.

In all tunes of this class, as, in fact, in all organ-music, great expertness in changing fingers upon one or more keys, as a preparation for notes that are immediately to follow, is absolutely necessary to a good legato style. This qualification forms a part of the technique presupposed in approaching the study of accompaniments. (See beginning of Preliminary Remarks.) Still, for the benefit of those who may be lacking in this respect, the following exercises are given here. They should be practiced at an extremely slow tempo at first, special care being taken that the finger-pairs fall simultaneously upon the keys.

EXAMPLE 8.

EXAMPLE 9.

EXAMPLE 10.

EXAMPLE 11.

Change of fingers upon the sharp keys.   When the change of fingers occurs upon the sharp keys with the fingering $\frac{5-4}{3-2}$ or $\frac{4-3}{2-3}$ it is impossible for the finger-pairs to fall quite simultaneously. In such cases, *in ascending passages, the lower finger of the two is first shifted,* followed instantly by the upper, thus:

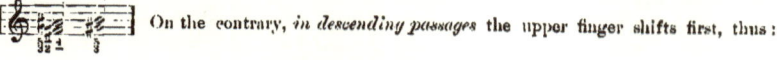 On the contrary, *in descending passages* the upper finger shifts first, thus:

One more example follows to illustrate distinctness in repeated notes or chords while preserving a strict legato. After having become familiar with Chapter III., it will be advantageous for the pupil to return to Example 12, and again practice it with reference to registration. Further examples of this class may readily be found in every church-book.

EXAMPLE 12.

Characteristics of the best Chorales.   The tunes thus far given have been selected solely to illustrate the reiteration of the same chord, so common in many tunes popular in America. The German chorales, and the better class of English choral tunes, will be found rarely to contain these repetitions, being infinitely richer and stronger in their harmonies. An example of each follows.

EXAMPLE 13.

Examination of this example shows at once the almost constant progression of the melody without syllabic repetition, producing a new chord to every syllable of the text. Compare this with the fifth measure of Example 1, the first measure of Example 6, etc. The student should not forget that the above notation ($\frac{4}{2}$—the ecclesiastical, so called) does not make the tempo slower, but, if any thing, rather quicker.

EXAMPLE 14.

London. C. M.   *Dr. Croft. 1700.*

Both of these examples are given *as sung.*

In Example 14, it will be noticed that not a single repetition of the kind under consideration occurs. This harmonic variety, as well as strength, makes this class of tunes not only more interesting musically, but also easier to play well. They agree with the character of the organ, and simply require good legato-playing, the tones which are common to any two chords *not being repeated.* It will be further noticed that the English tune is written without pauses (⌒). A slight (breathing) pause does, however, take place at the end of each line of the four-line stanza, but trifling as compared with the German chorale. This arises partly from the custom, prevalent in Germany, of singing a long hymn continuously, but with an extremely short interlude (or modulation to the following phrase) *between the lines*, not between the stanzas. The interlude, coming in this place, has the practical object of insuring unity between congregation and accompanist—the congregation singing the melody only. Thus a fresh start is obtained, no unimportant matter when a large congregation is singing with full voice. It may be interesting to the student to compare this simple church-setting of Example 13 with Mendelssohn's more elaborate harmonization, he having introduced this ancient melody as the first chorale in "St. Paul."

CHAPTER III.

OF ADDING AND WITHDRAWING STOPS DURING PERFORMANCE.

THE above subject is here introduced before proceeding to the consideration of more elaborate forms of accompaniment, as it comes into play to a good extent with the plain choral-tunes, and is indispensable in properly rendering music of a more varied character.

Combination Pedals. Modern organs, even the smaller ones, are usually provided with more or less " combination-pedals " for bringing on and taking off the more powerful stops. Some instruments (generally of the larger class) are, instead of this, or in addition thereto, appointed with " pneumatic knobs or buttons " placed between the Manuals. These, when touched by the thumb, accomplish the same purpose.

No matter how well provided an instrument may be in this respect, the effect produced is that of a *fixed combination*, and, especially in case of small or medium-sized instruments, is decidedly radical in its character—that is, the relative power passes at once from *piano* or *mezzo-piano* to *fortissimo* and *vice versa*. On the other hand, the accompanist may desire but a slight increase or decrease of tone, or it may be that he wishes to gain or reject a certain *quality* of tone not included in the stops affected by the combination-pedal.

Freeing the Hands. For these reasons, the organist can not dispense with studies which teach him how to free the hands alternately, if it be but for a moment, for the purpose of drawing on or pushing in a register. This also holds good should his particular instrument chance to be extraordinarily-provided with mechanical means of registration. To gain the technique requisite to thus make free either hand at pleasure, the first thing to acquire is dexterity in substituting one hand for another upon the same or succeeding chord.

Use of the Pedals when the left hand is made free. As a matter of course, removing the left hand from the manual leaves to the feet the whole duty of providing the bass part. Here we have the best proof that some proficiency in obligato pedal-playing is indispensable, even to the pupil whose ambition is limited to playing the plainest church-tunes *well*.

In case the pedals are being employed an octave lower than the vocal bass (see Example 2), it is generally preferable to play them *as written, while the left hand is thus removed*, that the distance between manual and pedal-tone may not be too great, and thus the blending of the two weakened or destroyed.

Substitution of Hands. In his own experience as a teacher, the author has found the following exercise to give the dexterity desired. We take as an illustration our former Example 6.

It is to be understood that no changes of stops are proposed in Example 15. For the moment, we have to do with nothing but the acquirement of such mechanical dexterity as is requisite to free a hand with which to make such changes subsequently.

EXAMPLE 15.

The alternation of hands is here far more frequent than would be required in a tune of this class for purposes of registration, but as a study it is all the better on this account.

In the second measure, the G of the left hand [music] and of the right [music] Continued Legato.

must be connected with each other, as also with the G of the first measure, so as to form together

the equivalent: [music]

This principle must be carefully observed throughout, in order that the ear may detect no break at the change of hands. Wherever the change occurs, the left hand inserts itself *over* the right.

It is evident that the tune must be played in *close* harmony to enable it to be treated thus, and the pupil should carefully compare this exercise with Example 6, measure for measure. Here, then, we see the necessity of a knowledge of the fundamental laws of harmony as to the inversions of chords, etc., as a preparation for the study of organ accompaniments. Assuming this (see close of Preliminary Remarks), we need not give further illustrations of the manner of freeing the hands, as the pupil can himself adapt a multitude of tunes to be treated in this way as studies until the required dexterity is attained.

Premising the mode of freeing the hands to have been thoroughly acquired, we now proceed to consider the subject proper of this chapter—namely, "adding and withdrawing stops during performance."

EXAMPLE 16.

In this example, we will suppose (1) the Gamba, or (2) the Stopped Diapason and Dulciana, or all three of these stops drawn upon the Great Organ. Let the pupil play the above, drawing with his right hand the following stops: at *a*, the Open Diapason, eight feet; at *b*, the Octave or Principal, four feet; and at *c*, the Twelfth and Fifteenth together. This increase of power might be carried further, but suffices to show a certain unsatisfactory abruptness of effect produced by the entrance of each stop. The same played backward, beginning with all the stops named and reducing them to the first combination, is nearly as unsatisfactory. The effect in Example 17 will be found to be much better.

EXAMPLE 17.

Let us analyze the reason of this:

A perfectly *even* crescendo, by means of adding stops, is, of course, unattainable from the varying character of the stops themselves. It will be found, however, that the abruptness of their entrance, before alluded to, can be greatly mitigated, and, under certain conditions, made to produce a positively good effect. In accompanying voices, these conditions mainly arise from the *sense or significance of the vocal text.* The following illustrations will give an idea of this:

EXAMPLE 18 (IN CRESCENDO: ADDING STOPS).

It is intended that the student add or withdraw the stops in these examples precisely as in Example 17 (with which example we would now compare Examples 18 and 19), carefully noting the significance of the words in connection with the accents produced.

In the first place, it will be noticed that the passage rises with the natural inflection of the words in Example 18, and falls on the same principle in Example

EXAMPLE 19 (IN DECRESCENDO: WITHDRAWING STOPS).

19; which is seen to be essentially Example 18 in reversed order.

It will also be noticed that the simple imitation occurring in the second measure of Example 18, materially strengthens the rhythm.

In Example 18 we find that the improved effect (as compared with Example 16) lies in one simple fact ; to which particular attention is called, as it contains the whole secret of adding and withdrawing stops properly—namely, *the stops are added or withdrawn upon the exact rhythmic accent of the piece.* Thus the added tone (by means of the added register) reinforces this natural accent, and the " too much " or " too little," which the character of the stop itself may produce, is not so keenly felt. It is the lack of agreement with this natural accent which partly accounts for the unpleasant effect of Example 16, the stop being there drawn upon the unaccented (weak) part of the measure. Example 16 is furthermore destitute of rhythmic accent and contains no harmonic changes. The reduction of tone produced by playing Example 16 backward is only rendered more tolerable by the fact that such reduction then falls upon the accented (strong) part of the measure. As it stands, the adding of stops produces a sort of syncopated accent upon the weak part of the measure.*

Agreement with the Rhythmic Accent.

Besides the good effect of agreement with the natural accent of a piece, it may be ascertained, by practical tests at the instrument, that where harmonies change at the moment of drawing the register the effect is improved and abruptness lessened. Care must be taken that the added register is heard promptly with the entrance of each new chord, and not with the expiration of the former one. Where a short series of staccato chords occur, it will be found still easier to produce a good effect, whether by way of increasing or decreasing the power.

Change of Harmonies ; Staccato.

In the illustrations given, a certain *radical* increase or decrease of power, coinciding with the natural accents of the measure and with the nature of the words, was intended. Thus, Example 18 adds (to the combination which begins the example) in quick succession the Open Diapason, eight feet, the Octave or Principal of four feet, and the Twelfth and Fifteenth, while Example 19 illustrates the reversed effect. .

Crescendo and Diminuendo by registration.

When, however, the problem proposed is to produce *as gradual* a crescendo or diminuendo as possible, and when this is to be accomplished without the aid of the Swell Organ, but by changes of registration, it is well to observe the following principles :

If we begin with a *piano* or *pianissimo* of the Great Organ—say the Stopped Diapason and Dulciana—it will be found that the latter stop may be added to the former with a less radical change of power and quality than if the order be inverted. The Open Diapason, eight feet, should not be added next. It is too powerful and radical in quality. If there is another stop of eight-foot flute-tone it should enter here. Then the Gamba or Salicional, which assimilates naturally with the stops already drawn, while it lends new power and pungency to the combination. Next the Flute of four feet. By this time a *mezzo-forte* power has been obtained, and the Open Diapason, being now added, is partially covered, and the radical character which would otherwise mark its entrance blended into that of general crescendo.

Order of Stop-addition, or the reverse.

The pupil should test this principle carefully, carrying it up to the use of the Full Organ with the manuals coupled. He will thereby ascertain that the most even crescendo is obtained by

---

* The above holds good when, as in Example 16, the power is reduced while *the same chord* continues sounding. This does not necessarily apply when the chords are varied. Cases will frequently occur where reducing the power upon the unaccented part of the measure will best carry out the sentiment expressed by the words, the weakened accent receiving the weakened power.

In adding stops, however, *the rule should be invariable*—namely, add upon the accented part of the measure only, unless a strong syncopated effect is intended. This is really no exception, as in such case the composer has transferred the place of the principal accent.

selection of stops from the different manuals at the outset, and not by gradually drawing all the stops of one manual and then proceeding to the next. As a matter of course, instruments of tolerably complete appointment are necessary to produce the effects described. In small organs it is often impossible to produce other effects than those here termed " radical."

From the preceding remarks, it should be evident that expertness in freeing the hands from the manuals, and thus being able to manipulate the registers, will find its greatest use in pieces of larger form and more artistic character than the plain tunes. Still, even in these the organist frequently desires to change the registration, moved thereunto either by (1) sentiment of the words, or (2) the fact that, in this country, a congregation commencing a tune rarely begin it " lustily and with a good courage," but gather increasing confidence and power as they proceed. Thus the last verse of a hymn will frequently require double the support which was ample for the first verse. We again recur to Example 6 as an illustration (somewhat exaggerated) of both crescendo and diminuendo in this sense.

EXAMPLE 20.

At the commencement of the tune by choir and congregation, we will suppose the accompaniment to consist of the eight-foot stops of the Great Organ (without reeds) coupled to Diapasons and Octave (four-foot) of the Swell, with the Pedal Organ properly balanced.

The organist frees his left hand at *a*, passing it over his right to the Great Organ registers, drawing the four-foot stops (Octave and Flute) exactly with *b*.

Here it will be noticed that the Pedal leaves the lower for the upper octave in order that the bass may not be too distant from the other parts.

At *c*, the hands shift upon the same chord, freeing the right hand to add the Twelfth and Fifteenth to the Great Organ at *d*.

At *e*, add Swell Reeds of eight feet (with Mixture *ad libitum*). An increase of power is preferable at this point, rather than with the entrance of the following measure, although that measure is the climax of the phrase, and where we might naturally expect the stop to be added.

The reason of the treatment proposed lies in the fact that the Soprano note ♮ at *e* is the leading tone to the dominant chord of G (D), and it is the tendency of voices to sing such leading tones (the major seventh of any key) a little below pitch, especially in a sustained movement. In fact, it might be preferable so to plan the order of increase as to bring on the Great Organ Twelfth and Fifteenth at this point, in order more successfully to combat this tendency, if it be found to exist, and thus secure the intonation.

At *f*, the left hand, passing to the Great Organ as at *a*, adds here the Trumpet of eight feet.

At *g*. For the three following measures, it is not advisable to add stops of greater power or higher pitch, as the tune here reaches the lowest point of its compass, and a range where female Soprano voices are particularly weak. In fact, this third strain would better serve as an illustration of diminuendo.

At *h*, the Great Organ Bourdon, or Open Diapason, of sixteen feet may be added. This does not materially add to the power already attained, but to the solidity of tone. In the use of manual-stops of sixteen feet, in accompanying choirs, great care and judgment must be exercised. This will be more particularly considered in treating of the accompaniment of the chant, although it also applies to the choral tunes. *Sixteen-foot Tone.*

The addition of the Double Diapason at *h* not only enriches the combination already arrived at, but also, by strengthening the foundation, justifies the addition of the Great Organ Mixtures at *i*.

The doubling of parts in both hands in this and the following measure is not to be considered as consecutive octaves. The four-part harmony is pure. The balance of the tune, namely, [musical notation] had better be treated in diminuendo. Such a reduction of the Great Organ may be effected thus: at 1, Mixture off; 2, Trumpet off; 3, Open Diapason, sixteen feet off (or Bourdon); 4, both Twelfth and Fifteenth off, the Swell being meantime closed. Should there be reason for a more sudden diminuendo, the following would answer: 1, Mixture and Trumpet off; 2, Twelfth and Fifteenth off; 3, Open Diapason, sixteen feet, or Bourdon off; 4, Swell Reeds and Mixtures off. In rapid diminuendos, stops may be removed on both the accented and unaccented parts of the measure. (See note, bottom of page 23.)

In church-playing, custom seems to have sanctioned beginning the tune by allowing the pedal-tone to be heard first before the chord is taken upon the manuals. The custom of slightly prolonging the pedal-note at the close of a piece prevails to a still greater extent. This seems to be justified on the ground that it is satisfactory to the ear to hear, at the last moment, the fundamental tone upon which the piece has been built up. In doing this, care must be taken to shut off the Pedal Coupler so that at the last moment the sixteen-foot tone only is heard. If stops of higher pitch (belonging to the Pedal Organ itself) have been drawn, they must be retired before the sixteen-foot tone ceases. *Pedal-note before and after the tune.*

Occasionally when a sort of "dying-away" effect, partly of the echo description, is desired from the Organ after the voices have ceased, it can be effectively accomplished thus: *Exceptional close.*

EXAMPLE 21.

* Voices cease here.

The left hand shifts to the Swell which enters unheard at 1, being covered by the Great Organ. At 2, the Pedal to Great Coupler should be withdrawn. This can only be done here by means of a pedal expressly for the purpose, with which nearly all modern instruments are provided. If the student's instrument unfortunately lacks this, the left hand must quickly remove the coupler before taking the chord upon the Swell. This treatment not unfrequently comes into play most usefully in accompaniment itself.

Stop and Swell diminuendo. Referring to Example 16 and the remarks that follow concerning diminuendo by means of stops, a few words may not be out of place here respecting an apparently similar instance in Example 21 at "3." Important differences will be detected on closer examination.

1. The chord is here sustained upon the Swell and not upon the Great Organ. The local position of the Swell Pipes within the Organ and their relative power produce far less abruptness in reducing the stops than in case of the Great Organ.

2. In Example 21, the sustained tone is supposed to come at the end of a piece where the rhythm has become firmly established, and the reduction of stops on the first beat of each measure serves to maintain that rhythm to the close.

3. The diminuendo of the Swell itself, by means of the Swell Pedal, both helps the rhythm, and, properly managed, checks possible abruptness.

"Downward roll."   EXAMPLE 22.

Coupler off.

This ending is given as nearly as may be expressed in notes, and may be termed the "downward roll," as the effect to be produced is not that of a measured arpeggio.

The chord must, as it were, sink away suddenly and disappear, leaving only the momentary prolongation of the pedal-tone. To this end, the fingers must be removed with rapidity and great precision.

This and the former example are given as illustrations of certain means employed to avoid an abrupt close, such as is produced by simultaneously taking hands and feet off the instrument, and are effects peculiar to the Organ. On the other hand, multitudes of examples might be cited where the abruptness of close referred to is precisely the effect to be sought for as characterizing the composition. One illustration of this will suffice.

EXAMPLE 23.

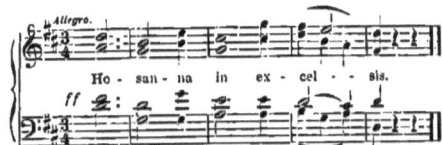

Ho - san - na in ex - cel - - sis.

In examples similar to this (the ending of the "Sanctus" of Mozart's Requiem Mass), any prolongation of tone, through a hold upon the pedal or otherwise, would be manifestly out of place.

The dexterity (which it is hoped this chapter will assist the student in acquir-

Judgment in application of means.

ing) might be carried to such a degree that a change of combination or effect might be possible in nearly every measure of a moderate movement. It must not be forgotten, however, that a realizing sense of varying conditions—in a word, good taste—governs the use of these means. This is the real artistic law, and no written studies, illustrations, nor even hearing good model performances, can teach it if the germ be not latent in the pupil. Thus it is a matter of course that effects like Examples 21 and 22 are not to be appended to the end of every or every other composition.

It now remains for the pupil, according to the measure of his talent, to make practical the hints that are contained in this chapter, by such practice as shall enable him to free either hand in all compositions of moderate difficulty and tempo.

CHAPTER IV.

ACCOMPANIMENT OF QUARTET CHOIRS.

Opposition to
Quartet
Choirs ; their
musical limi-
tation.
AT a recent clerical convocation, one of the reverend delegates remarked, in effect, that
" America was the only country on the face of the globe where churches entrusted their songs
of praise to four individuals." This is unfortunately the fact, although the true reason for
deprecating it does not lie *merely* in the theological idea which the speaker had in mind; for,
it might be replied, that many of our denominations delegate their prayers to one individual,
who may or may not represent the aspirations of his hearers. At all events, opposition to quartet
choirs may be based upon purely musical grounds. Quartet singing *alone* narrows down the
scope of much good music composed for church service, and excludes the possibility of much
contrast in musical effect. It suffers especially from being incapable of those large, dignified
effects which are within the scope of even a moderate-sized chorus. We do not propose,
however, to argue the much-discussed topic of Quartet *versus* Chorus Choirs. We have simply
to deal with the fact that the former exist, and, whatever the signs of the future may be, they
unfortunately form at present the majority.

Difference
of treatment
required.
To accompany them properly requires different modes of treatment, and this treatment
(as a matter of study) finds constant use in the accompaniment of Anthems. The class of tunes
especially appropriate to Quartet use requires far more dexterity in handling the instrument
than the plain Chorales. It is evident that when only four voices are employed, individual
defects or weaknesses are easily noted. Thus it becomes here the peculiar duty of the organist
to conceal or overcome the same, as far as may be, through his playing. On the other hand,
individual singers have individual merits as well as defects. These merits of voice and style
need to be placed in a favorable light, so as to be recognized as such, and to this end a good
accompanist contributes much. Neither does singer nor player, in thus presenting the best points
of his or her talent for the benefit of the sanctuary, necessarily do any thing out of consonance with
the place or occasion. A large majority of the individuals who constantly have the quotation,
" Sing with the spirit," upon their tongues, fail to complete the text, " and with the
understanding also." Thus the conditions of accompanying a few voices, in music of a more
elaborate character than that already considered, become a matter of far greater intricacy.
This is true to such an extent that we must content ourselves with but comparatively few hints,
where we would gladly say much under less varying conditions—trusting that the pupil's talent
may be such as to bear much fruit from but little seed here sown.

N. B.—It must not be forgotten that much that is classified, for convenience' sake, under Classification. *other heads, will be found to bear upon the subject of Quartet accompaniment with nearly the same significance as the suggestions which immediately follow.*

It is useless to attempt to draw the exact line which shall divide tunes suited to Quartet from those adapted to Chorus Choirs. It will depend largely upon the training and natural voices of a given Chorus Choir as to how far its repertory may encroach upon that of the Quartet. In general, however, the *character* of the tune may be said to govern this quite as much as the relative difficulty. Thus the following example, although simple, is essentially a quartet tune, and would lose rather than gain in character if sung by a chorus:

EXAMPLE 24 (AS WRITTEN AND SUNG).

We now give one of the many possible forms of accompanying the above, that the reader, having it before his eyes, may consider with us the points that follow:

EXAMPLE 25.

Variation of the Accompaniment from the written form of the tune.

At *a*, comparing Examples 24 and 25, we see that the Soprano begins thus:  which thematic bit is repeated frequently in different forms throughout the tune. Now, few Sopranos will give this and its repetition with perfect accuracy as to time in every instance (nor is it necessary), but will make it sometimes [♪] and again [♪] approximately. In a word, even the practised accompanist will find a difficulty in passing from the note *c* to *d* precisely with the singer, but may still be holding the *c* when the singer passes to *d*, or, on the contrary, may anticipate the voice.

Although a slight matter in one sense, and frequently unperceived by the player seated at the keys, yet the farther off in the building (that is, reasonably so) the critical listener is removed, the more apparent becomes the discrepancy.

The treatment given at *a*, Example 25, will wholly obviate this, and the other points in the tune where the same principle obtains will be easily recognized by comparison with Example 24.

A subdued accompaniment is, of course, assumed, whereby the *melodic* difference with the Soprano is not perceived, while the *harmonic* support to the voices remains the same.

"Pedal abuse."

At *b*, we call attention to the pedals being unemployed, and the bass played upon another manual with a register (or registers) of eight feet. Here a few words as to what may be termed *pedal abuse.*

A young organist, especially if he has begun to acquire some pedal execution, seeing the pedals and their stops before him, is very apt to think that they are there for use, and accordingly uses them (that is, the sixteen-foot stops) *all the time.* This is very faulty, especially in Quartet accompaniment, besides being opposed to all principles of contrast. These deep basses, continuously employed, weary the ear, and impart a heaviness to the performance which should by no means characterize it. Besides, these low tones are of incomparable effect when they are introduced *after* a certain continuance of eight-foot tone.

Employment of eight-foot Manual Stops in the lower octave instead of the Pedal.

In addition to this cessation of all pedal tone, it must also be noted, and practically tested, that many of the eight-foot stops used in the lower octave (thus giving the sixteen-foot tone as compared with the vocal notation) will have a much better effect in Quartet accompaniment than using the pedal sixteen-foot stops *as the notation stands*, and an infinitely better effect than the same employed in the lower octave. The reason of this will be found in the fact that the eight-foot stops of the manual, employed in the lower octave, give a more delicate foundation than the sixteen-foot stops used in the upper (pedal) octave. The eight-foot stops have weight enough to serve as a foundation in tunes of this class. They assimilate better with the *single* bass voice, which by this treatment is left to move freely within its own octave. Lastly, they are more definite in their quality, viewed as a means of accompaniment of this class of tunes. There is no objection to the use of the *pedal key-board*, for convenience' sake, in such cases, provided that the manuals are coupled with it and the sixteen-foot stops withdrawn.

Manual-bass in octaves.

At *c*, the left hand gives the octave instead of the single tone, in order to assure the intonation of the bass voice. The fall of the diminished, following the perfect, fourth (*a—e* and *f—c* ♮) is somewhat difficult, especially if the voice be ponderous, or if the singer has a cold—is "out of voice," etc.

This leads us to speak of a more radical mode of assistance in such a case as that presupposed, and is to be taken as an exception.

EXAMPLE 26.

Here the right hand plays the accompaniment upon the Choir Melodia (or the Great Organ Dulciana or Stopped Diapason). The pedals are coupled to the Choir or Great Organ with a soft Pedal Bourdon or Dulciana, sixteen feet, drawn. At the critical points *a* and *b*, the organist places his left hand upon the Swell which has a reed-stop drawn (Oboe or Trumpet of eight feet). The entrance of this new quality of tone will almost always restore a wavering intonation—otherwise the case is hopeless. It is to be understood that the entrance of the reed tone is to be qualified as to power by the use of the Swell-Pedal, so that its entrance be not too abrupt. Once heard, however, the reed tone must, for the sake of symmetry, be carried through the phrase, as far as *d*, Example 25.

At *c*, Example 25, the Pedal sixteen feet may be added preliminary to the following crescendo. Coming here upon the unaccented part of the measure, it forms no real exception to the principles laid down for adding stops. Here it gives, thus drawn, a melodic figure, namely,

besides not being open to the objection which occurs when stops of higher pitch are added against the rhythmic accent.

At *f*, compare with Example 24. The moving quarter-notes in the accompaniment do not here conflict with the Soprano, as they belong to the same chord.

At *g*, it will be noticed that the accompaniment sustains, while the melody moves.

At *h*, the accompaniment moves (within the chord), while the melody sustains. Such treatment is preferable in many cases to actual progression with the voices, often lending both fulness and steadiness to the effect.

Turning to the third strain of Example 24, it will be seen that the Tenor voice repeats seven times the tone *C*, and that in a sustained movement. This is simplicity itself to the eye, and at an easy part of the Tenor compass. It is none the less true that many of our Tenor friends find just such a prolongation of a given tone difficult to sing in tune—the difficulty probably lying in the shifting harmonies around them while they have the inner part. Calling the singer's attention to this will not unfrequently cause him to *sing it worse* through nervousness. The accompanist may help him thus : Assisting the Tenor intonation.

EXAMPLE 27.

or the Great Organ stop may be first introduced later. If immediately before the B♮, the cadence must be completed. (See Example 24.)

Again recurring to the third strain of Example 24, we find what may be termed a *natural* crescendo and diminuendo. There may be other shades of expression elsewhere, but in nearly every tune of this class we find some one strain where the crescendo and decrescendo seem the only natural expression Of adaptation of Words to the Music. of the phrase. Such is the third strain of Example 24. We would call the attention of students to the fact that where such crescendos or decrescendos occur—and as a rule, with exceptions, they will be found when voices rise to a higher part of their compass—all adaptations of words to such tunes must follow suit and increase in emotional intensity. As regards accent, the words must yield to the music in every case, for the simple reason that the music *can not* yield to the words. We may vary inflection and accent to a good degree in reading without materially injuring the sense. On the other hand, the musical phrase, as it stands written, is inflexible. The rule to be deduced from this is a simple one—" See to it that, in adaptation of words to tunes, or tunes to words, they *do* agree." A " Long-metre" tune and " Long-metre" verse may even agree perfectly as to general sentiment, the number of notes may coincide perfectly with the number of syllables, and yet be faulty as to accents common to both. This fault, which unfortunately can not be wholly rectified in the setting of our hymns to music, might be greatly modified for the better if organists and choir-directors would but give more time and thought to the subject. This comes, properly enough, under the head of " Quartet tunes," as the discrepancy alluded to will be more frequently noticed and felt in tunes of this class. Example 24 may be considered a good adaptation. Sentiment of words and style of music certainly agree, but we will give the second verse of this hymn, and it will be seen that the adaptation is not perfect. For brevity's sake, we simply give the melody.

EXAMPLE 28.

At * the music makes a complete cadence, closing in the tonic. This corresponds literally with the period in punctuation. But neither period nor comma occurs in the text at this point, so that the sentiment expressed is equivalent to " My heart kindles with a pure desire to see thy face," etc. It is the so-called half or dominant cadence which is here wanted in the music to make it approach a true rendering of the text ; and yet the above is by no means so aggravated a specimen as many that occur. This is the fault into which some uneducated (and therefore " would-be") composers fall in setting the words of the *Te Deum*—" To Thee, Cherubim and Seraphim continually do cry," with a complete cadence (period), or a " deceptive" one to the minor, as if it were a matter of *grief* instead of a declaration that " Cherubim and Seraphim continually do cry, Holy !" etc.

Relations of Musical Cadences to punctuation of text.

The young accompanist, who really wishes to excel, will find in the words themselves most useful hints as regards adaptation and registration.

Several tunes of " quartet" character follow, which it is hoped will find practical use, as well as illustrate the subject.

EXAMPLE 29.

Example 29, *a.*—The accompaniment given in the first and second measures is preferable to playing the voice parts literally, as it allows the Soprano perfect freedom of utterance in these two measures. The registration should at first be very light, just enough to secure the intonation: Swell, Stopped Diapason, and Salicional, for instance, or the latter only. If the Swell contains a divided Bourdon (which should always be the case if the Swell has a sixteen-foot stop allotted to it), the "Bourdon-Bass" should also be drawn. As the division of the stop occurs at "four-foot C" (first bass note of Example 29), the sixteen-foot tone will not be given by the Bourdon Bass

Value of a *divided* Bourdon in the Swell Organ.

during the first two measures, as the downward compass of the divided stop begins with the half-step below this note. At the G (third measure), a delicate sixteen-foot tone will make itself heard in the bass only, and, coinciding with the change of harmony to the dominant seventh, is of extremely good effect. This can not be produced if the Bourdon is undivided, as the stop would then affect the whole manual range. This division of the Swell sixteen-foot stop is exceedingly valuable in soft effects where a low bass is required, producing a more delicate tone than the pedal-stops of sixteen feet.

At *b*, the Pedal sixteen-foot tone enters for two measures to assist the crescendo. It also offers opportunity to free the left hand if necessary, although the Swell Pedal may furnish sufficient crescendo here. For the contrary reason, the Pedal ceases during the last two measures of this strain.

At *c*, the Pedal again resumes, giving the left hand ample opportunity to add stops preparatory to and during the coming crescendo.

Balance in crescendo obtained through a certain use of Swell Pedal.

In this connection, the pupil should become expert in the following exercise, which will be often found useful in passages of this kind. Suppose the Swell half open, the right hand upon the key-board, the left upon the register to be added to the first combination. As the stop is drawn, simultaneously meet it with the Swell Pedal, *closing* the Swell more or less in proportion to the power of the stop added. Reeds will require the most on account of their quality. Thus the closing of the Swell balances to a good extent the addition of the stop or stops, and affords subsequent opportunity for further crescendo by means of the Swell Pedal. Of course every advantage that can be afforded the rhythmic entrance of stops, according to the suggestions of Chapter III., must here be employed.

At *d*, the remarks governing the form of accompaniment at *a* hold good.

At *e*, the Great to Pedal Coupler is drawn—the Great Organ having been previously prepared with, say Open and Stopped Diapasons, and possibly Flute, four feet. At this point, it is evident that the bass only will be affected by the Great Organ (through the Coupler), making clear the chromatic progression of the bass. Should a very sudden and powerful crescendo be required, drawing the stops might be reserved until this point, *e*. The Swell would then be opened rhythmically, and the stops likewise added on each of the four beats of the measure, thus:

At *f*, the Pedal Organ may be strengthened by the addition of the powerful Double Diapason, sixteen feet.

Climax and Diminuendo.

At *g* occurs the climax. The left hand passes to the Great Organ at the last quarter-note of the previous measure, and at *g* takes a full chord. This chord is not to be held out as its notation would indicate, but is to disappear at once in a "downward roll." (See Chapter III., remarks under Example 22.)

At *h*, the right foot closes the Swell instantly upon the conclusion of this "roll" (which must be cut short), while the left hand shuts off the Pedal Double Diapason, and reduces the Swell rapidly to *piano*. This may seem a good deal to do within the limits of one or, at the most, two measures. The movement, however, is slow, and no great amount of practice will make such a diminuendo seem like child's play upon an organ with which the player is familiar. The effect is certainly excellent if smoothly done.

It must not be forgotten that these are not effects in *solo-playing*, but that the voices continue meantime, and do not make any thing like so sudden a decrescendo. Consequently they aid in equalizing the effect to the listener at a distance. On the one hand, they cover possible abruptness in the accompanimental treatment; on the other, the accompaniment yields to the purely vocal effect, the climax-point once passed.

Qualifying effect of the Voices upon the Accompaniment.

The mental conception of how a given organ combination sounds at a distance from the keys—whether in vocal combination or by itself—must be acquired by every good accompanist. Some instruments "carry over," as it is termed, when the pipes produce their true effect at some distance from the instrument. Of such organs it is safe to say, that in many pieces of a soft character, voices and accompaniment only sound perfectly balanced (to the congregation) when the accompanist hears but an occasional note of his instrument or literally nothing.

Conception of organ effect remote from the player.

EXAMPLE 30.

The accompaniment to Example 30, as here experimentally given, leads to the following comments:

Accent.   The registration, as in the previous example, should be quite subordinate to the voices at the beginning of the tune. At *a*, it will be noticed that the Pedal enters on the accent of the first full measure, and not on the previous quarter-note. This is in order to help the accent, with which the tune may properly be said to begin.

In the second stanza, we have an illustration of that disagreement (already alluded to) between the accent of the musical phrase and that of the words. This is too frequently allowed to occur in adaptation of hymns to music. (See comments to Example 28.)

The natural accent of this stanza is, "*Arm* me with jealous care." As forced by the music, it becomes, "Arm *me*," etc. This, as an expression of individual feeling, might possibly be allowed to remain in this instance. At all events, it may easily be rectified, by letting the voices

begin with the full measure, thus:

          Arm me with jeal - ous care,

This, on the other hand, would give an impossible accentuation for the first verse. Where such discrepancies occur, the tune should be carefully examined to see if a slight omission, like the previous instance, will not help the case.

At Example 28, it will be noted that the cause of disagreement was a *harmonic* one—produced by the complete cadence of the music to an unfinished sentence of the text. In Example 30, the disagreement is purely *melodic*—produced by simple accentuation.

At *b*, we have a crescendo, accomplished both by the Swell Pedal and by the addition of stops to the Swell, if desired. The left hand is freed for this purpose by taking the passage in close harmony. This is a good example of what we have termed "natural crescendo." (See comments on Example 24, but following Example 27.) It will be observed that this particularly suits the sentiment of the first stanza—the second to a less degree.

At *c*, the Pedal ceases, together with the harmonics of the right hand. Here the peculiar acceleration (*not of tempo*) of the voices, by means of notes of lesser value, is such that the execution of this passage by good singers will sound at once freer and more concise, if virtually unaccompanied. The organist has, meantime, an opportunity to reduce the Swell combination. Without accompaniment.

At *d*, the organist merely *supports* the voices, not playing their parts in unison. It is simply absurd to attempt to follow voices in a passage like this. The combined result would very rarely be a united one, nor, if it were so, would the effect be as good. The voices should be left in absolute freedom as to melodical progression, but supported harmonically. Singers who can not execute such a passage in tune, etc., without having their parts literally played (rehearsals possibly excepted), have no business to sing such tunes at all. Even the four voices must not execute the first half of this measure slavishly in time. The Tenor must adapt himself to the Soprano as in a duet, and Alto and Bass watch, and listen carefully to the other two parts. Of support without playing the voice-parts.

At *e*, the chord is taken in the accompaniment in preference to the single (bass) tone, on account of the slight break, made by all the voices here taking breath in anticipation of the coming phrase.

At *f*, the crescendo effect will have to be principally accomplished by the voices, as the Swell has now been reduced to *pp* as to stops, as well as closed. Besides this, the same soft accompaniment is required in the following phrase. Upon a three-manual Organ the half measure preceding *e* (with the following chord) may be taken upon the Choir Dulciana. While the Choir Organ is thus employed, a few stops may be added to the Swell, which is resumed at, and can thus support, the crescendo of the following phrase. In this case the line, " My calling to fulfil," may again be played upon the Choir Organ, and the Swell resumed at *g*.

At *g*; if the Organ has but two manuals, stops may be added to the Swell, not only upon the accent of the measure, but also upon each of the three quarter-notes. (See Example 29, under *e*.)

At *h*, the decrescendo at the close of the previous phrase having been accomplished by gradually closing the Swell, the organist has now opportunity to reduce the stops likewise. He may even shut off the most powerful stop (of the combination supposed to be drawn at present) at the beginning of the previous measure, as the tone *E* is doubled and can be omitted from the Tenor-part.

The voices had better be left to themselves here, for reasons virtually similar to those stated at *d*.

The single *pianissimo* chord introduced in this measure (*h*), is for the purpose of insuring (not restoring) the intonation. This the soft manual-bass already aids to a good extent. In such cases the accompanist, one of whose first requisites is a good ear, must listen intently, and if the voices are not in the most perfect tune, such a chord is, of all things, that which he must avoid introducing. A bad case of " out of tune" is not supposed, but a " suspicion" of a downward tendency. Should such occur, the comparative remoteness of the accompanying bass—especially with a soft-manual Bourdon—renders this less noticeable. The possible means by which an accompanist may help singers in case of false intonation will be considered subsequently under the head of the Swell Organ. (Chapter X., page 116.) Intonation.

Example 31 (7s double.)

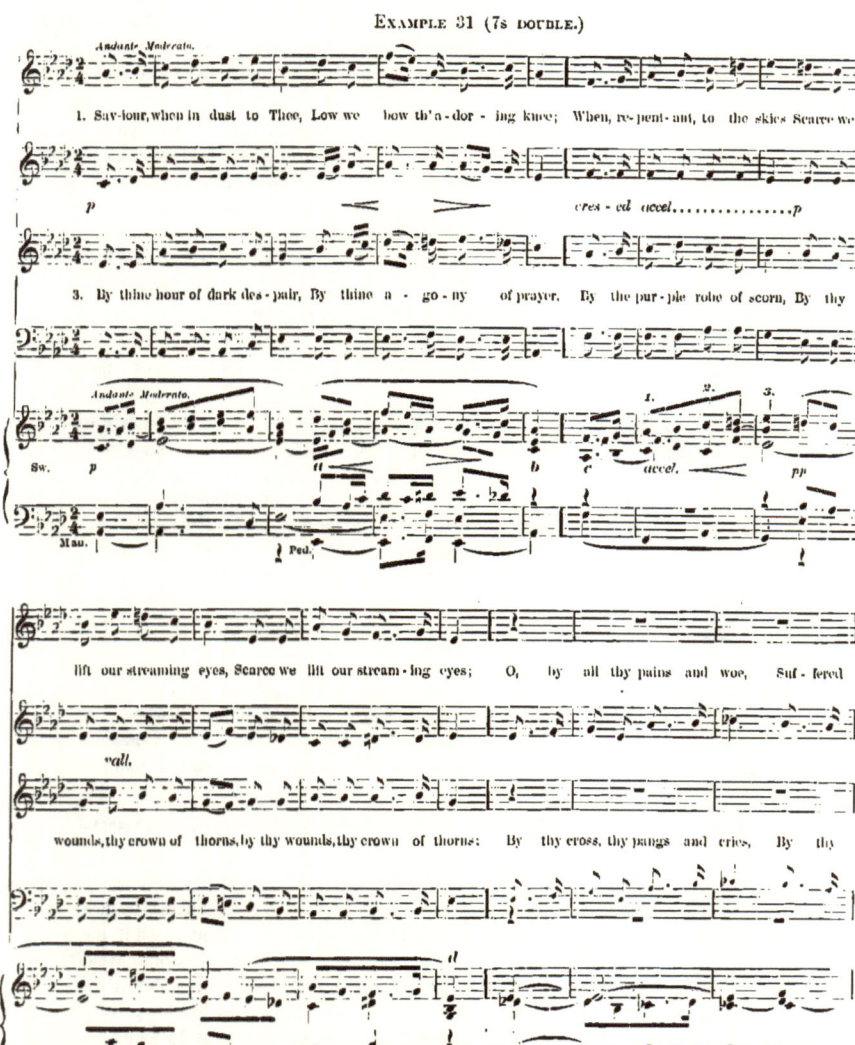

Arr. from R. Franz.

once for man be-low, Bending from thy throne on high, Hear our solemn lit - a - ny,...... Hear our solemn lit - a - ny.

cres. e poco accel.   *pp*   *roll*

per-fect sac-ri-fice: Je-sus, look with pity-ing eye, Hear our solemn lit - a - ny....... Hear our solemn lit - a - ny.

f   *g*   *h*   Adagio.   *pp*

cres. e poco accel.

Ped.   Man.

Example 31.—The accompaniment here begins in close harmony. This form was necessitated by the wish to begin with eight-foot stops only, without pedals, and thus to avoid the stretch of a tenth (A flat to C), which would occur in the third chord of the first full measure. The pedals are supposed to be coupled to the Swell, and possibly to the Great Organ Stopped Diapason; if a three-manual Organ, to the Choir Melodia in preference. *No* Pedal-stop is supposed drawn at first. (In this connection, see again Example 25, note *b*.)

At *b*, Example 31; the right hand assuming the harmony, the left passes quickly to the Pedal Bourdon or Dulciana of sixteen feet, which is drawn at *c*.

As the opening registration was very light, and the Swell is now closed from the diminuendo preceding *b*, stops may be added respectively at the figures 1, 2, 3, together with a crescendo, by means of the Swell Pedal. Whether an addition at 1 or 1, 2 (without that at 3) will or will not prove sufficient, depends upon the voices accompanied and the character of the instrument employed. The Swell is quickly closed at the *pianissimo* following 3.

At *d*, the right hand again assuming the harmony, the Swell-stops can be reduced, if necessary, for the accompaniment of the solo voice which follows.

At *e*, the Pedal resuming (now with the sixteen feet already drawn), enables the left hand to add stops at the points *f* and *g*.

At *h*, the diminuendo begins immediately after striking the chord. It must be gradual, however, and may terminate with the "downward roll" previously referred to. In such case the lower B flat may be added to the chord. Care should be taken if the "roll" is here introduced, that it terminates promptly with the voices.

At *i*, the following manner of closing is suggested, as good in many cases of a *pianissimo* ending where the voices have been heard without accompaniment immediately previous.

During the preceding rests the organist reduces the Swell to Stopped Diapason only. The Swell is, of course, wholly closed. The *right hand* plays the low E flat, the left resting in

Pianissimo sixteen-foot ending.

readiness upon the Bourdon register of the Swell. This stop is drawn simultaneously with the sixteenth note that follows. As the voices die away, the Stopped Diapason is shut off, leaving the Bourdon to linger alone for an instant. The effect of this addition of sixteen-foot tone and subsequent withdrawal of eight feet may be thus expressed :   The notes

played are those of Example 31. In some organs, it might be preferable to take the Bourdon at once, which would then be played :

EXAMPLE 32 (8s AND 7s DOUBLE).

Example 31.—In the beginning of this tune, the Pedal Bourdon is supposed to be coupled to the Swell.

At *a*, the Great to Pedal Coupler is to be drawn. If the Organ possess no mechanical means of doing this, the harmony easily admits of three parts being here played by the right hand, thus freeing the left hand for this purpose.

At *b*, both hands change to the Great Organ, which must be registered not to exceed *mezzo-forte* (that is, *mezzo-forte* as accompaniment for four voices), and coupled with the Swell.

At *c*, on removing the hands from the Great Manual, the Pedal Coupler to the same is removed. The accompaniment then returns to the Swell for the decrescendo and the following phrase.

At *d*, the Pedal is used to end the phrase, but, it will be remembered, is coupled only with the Swell.

At *e*, the vocal bass is supported by the manual octaves, the Pedal being reserved for the following crescendo.

At *f*, close harmony is employed, at which point the Pedal Open Diapason, sixteen feet, is added for the coming *forte* passage, and the Pedal to Great Coupler added. The hands then pass to the Great Organ, the asterisks * * * denoting a sudden reduction of stops of both Great and Swell. The manner of accomplishing this has already been treated of. The left hand can be spared for the purpose, as will be seen.

The Pedal Open Diapason, sixteen feet, is also shut off at the beginning of the fourth measure of this phrase.

At *g*, the *left hand* passes to the Swell at the moment the last chord is played upon the Great Organ. This is an application in accompaniment of Example 21, Chapter III.

Lack of space forbids our accompanying the following tunes with suggestive comments. If, however, we have been successful in making clear the points at issue in the examples thus far given, the student should now experience no difficulty in finding a suitable form of accompaniment and mode of registration for them. It should not be forgotten that the form of accompaniment given in the previous examples is by no means the only correct one.* It is just this possible elasticity of treatment which makes the study interesting, profitable, and artistic.

Recapitulation. To recapitulate: besides considering the character of the voices to be accompanied, and the characteristic virtues or vices of the particular instrument at his command, the accompanist should carefully observe the sentiment of the words, their accent and varying inflections. This last item furnishes, in almost every case, a key to the required manner of performance. This is the reason why so many persons of limited execution, but of true æsthetic taste, really accompany *well*, and would accompany *better* if they possessed more technique. This is to be acquired by organ studies proper, and forms the broad foundation upon which the whole structure must rest.

This also solves the mystery why so many players of marked executive attainments are rather dreaded than desired as accompanists by singers.

Mental requisites. In Art, as in other matters, "union is strength"—that is, union of technique with taste. Technique, if lacking, may in most instances be acquired under proper instruction. Taste, if latent, must develop itself. It can not, properly speaking, be taught, but only influenced. The first requisite to its development is an active mind, and, as far as our work is concerned, complete freedom from the idea that the more notes control the manner of an accompaniment in Church Music.

In the musical service of the church, the Organ is supposed to accompany and support the voices, not the voices the Organ. Too many of our accompanists seem to be laboring under the delusion that the latter relation is the proper one. In this connection, it may be said that *in a crescendo* the effect is often good when, *for a moment*, at a climax, the Organ exceeds due proportions as an accompaniment, but it must instantly subside.

The normal condition in an accompaniment must be artistic subordination, and is especially to be observed in accompanying a quartet of voices.

EXAMPLE 33 (8s AND 7s).

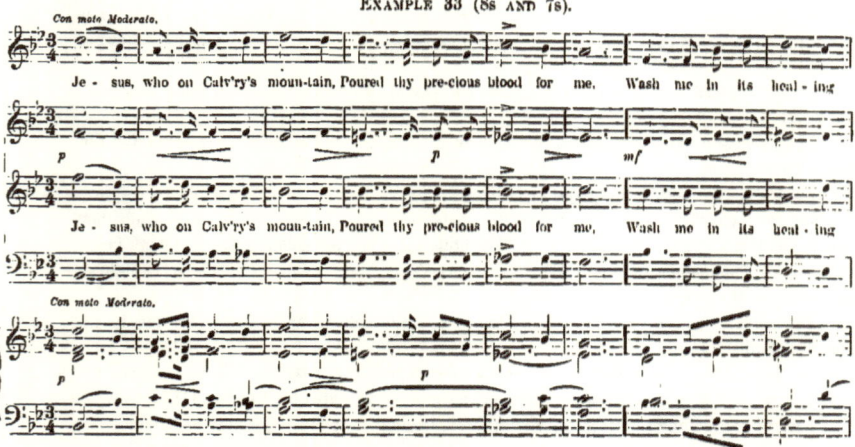

Je - sus, who on Calv'ry's moun-tain, Poured thy pre-cious blood for me, Wash me in its heal - ing

Je - sus, who on Calv'ry's moun-tain, Poured thy pre-cious blood for me, Wash me in its heal - ing

*In the following examples, the accompaniment given is, with few exceptions, merely the compressed voice parts. It does not then govern the *form and manner of execution*, which is left to the performer to adapt after the manner of the previous examples.

* Accompaniment should not move with Soprano.

EXAMPLE 34.

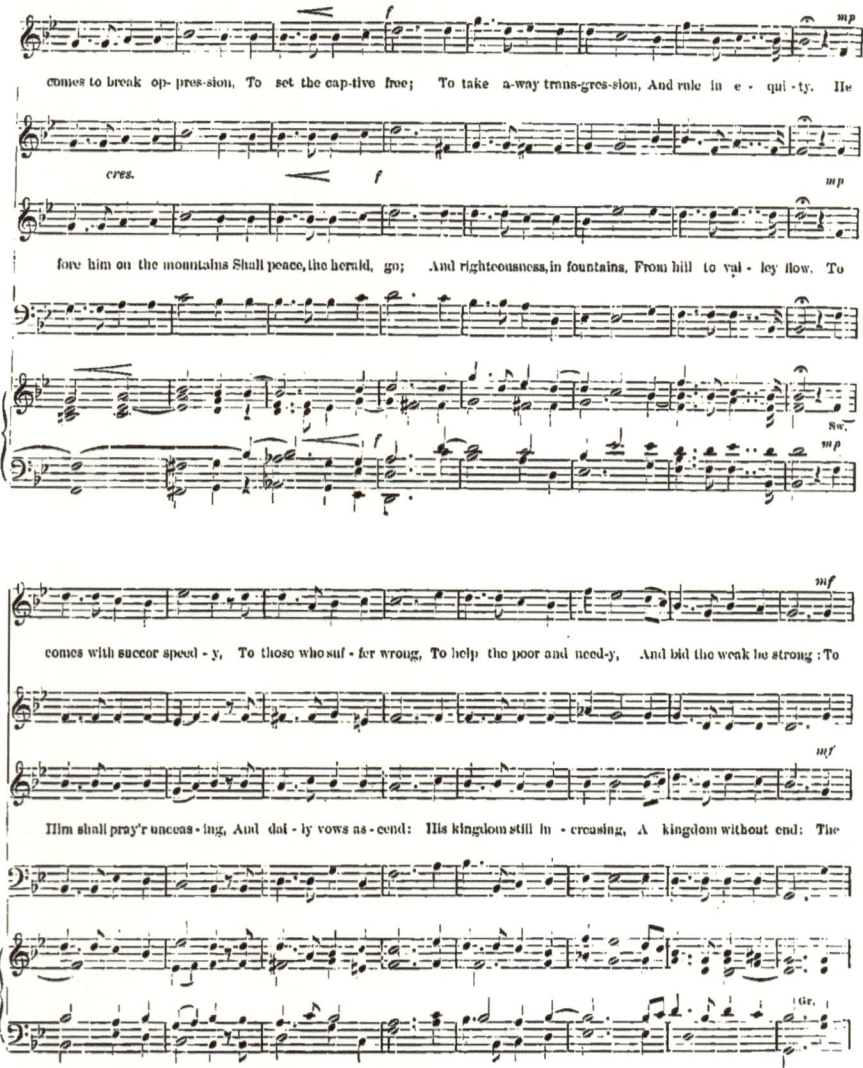

comes to break op-pres-sion, To set the cap-tive free; To take a-way trans-gres-sion, And rule in e - qui-ty. He

fore him on the mountains Shall peace, the herald, go; And righteousness, in fountains, From hill to val - ley flow. To

comes with succor speed - y, To those who suf - fer wrong, To help the poor and need-y, And bid the weak be strong : To

Him shall pray'r unceas - ing, And dai - ly vows as - cend; His kingdom still in - creasing, A kingdom without end: The

give them songs for sighing, Their darkness turn to light, Whose souls condemn'd and dying, Were pre-cious in His sight.

tide of time shall nev-er His cov-e-nant re-move, His name shall stand for-ev-er, That Name to us is love.

EXAMPLE 35 (L. M. 6 LINES).

1. As pant-ing in the sul-try beam, The hart de-sires the cool-ing stream, So to thy pres-ence,

4. Ah why, by pass-ing clouds op-prest, Should vex-ing tho'ts dis-tract thy breast? Turn, turn to Him in

48

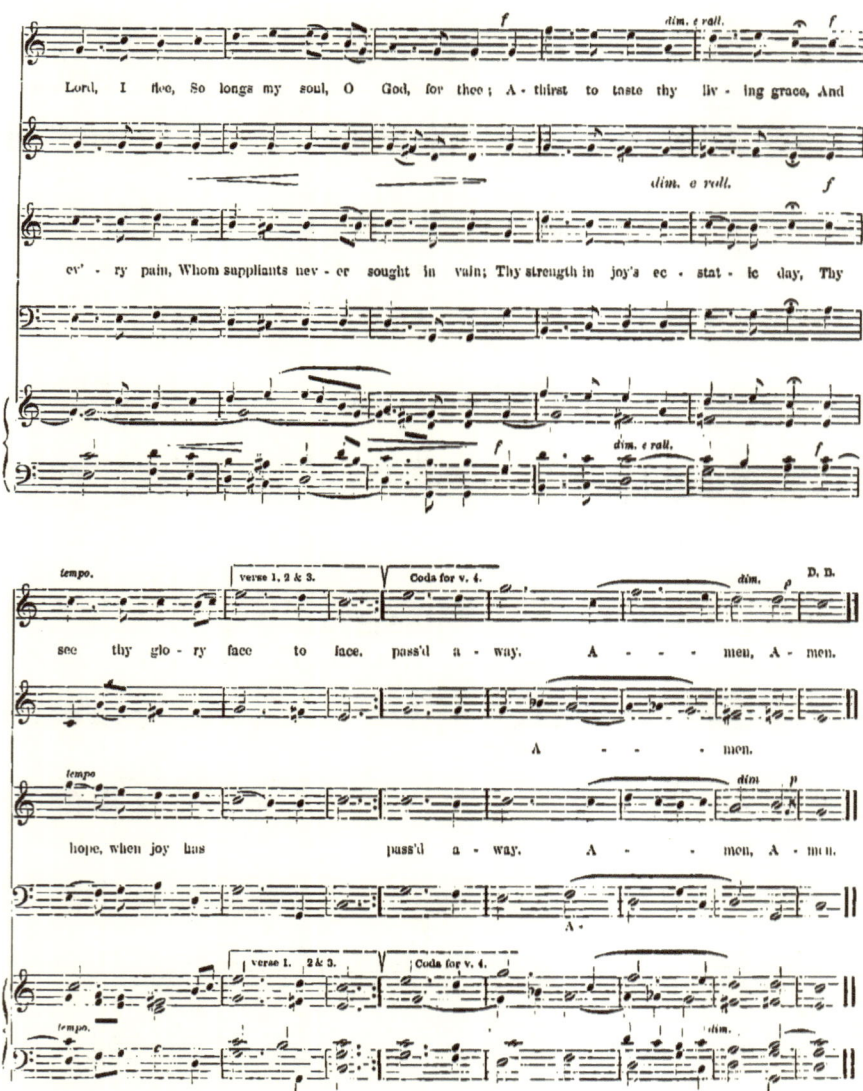

EXAMPLE 36 (8s AND 7s).

1. Bless'd be thou, the God of Is - rael, Thou, our Fa - ther, and our Lord;

2. Thine, O Lord, are power and great - ness, Glo - ry, vic - t'ry are thine own;

Bless'd thy Ma - jes - ty.... for - ev - er, Ev - er be..... thy name a - dored.

All is thine in earth and hea - ven, O - ver all thy bound - less throne.

In closing this chapter, a few words may not be amiss respecting an accomplishment which is extremely useful in quartet and solo accompaniment, but is unfortunately but little cultivated. We refer to Transposition.

Transposition.

When four persons constitute the choir, it would seem necessary that each one should always be "in voice." This, however, is rather the exception than the rule, especially in winter-time in our variable climate.

The organist should be able to assist the singers in performing their duty under such, to them, trying circumstances.

Let a Soprano or Tenor (these two voices more especially, except in case of Alto or Bass solos) come to church with a slight cold. The transposition of a given piece a half step lower may, under such circumstances, insure the performance of it *in tune*, when otherwise the result would be lamentable.

Ascertaining the Pitch required by certain voices. Again, let two quartet choirs of apparently equal ability as to vocal compass, quality of voices, etc., perform the same tune in the same key, one will frequently (perhaps we may say usually) harmonize better together than the other.

Now, transpose the tune a half step higher or lower for the inferior quartet, and the result is that it frequently sounds as well or better than the first quartet. This shows that a *certain* key fits a *certain* tune for *certain* voices. To discover this key is the duty of the organist in tunes of this class. It may very likely be the case that the key as written is the proper one, but the *fact* remains to be ascertained. This principle also obtains in accompanying congregational singing, many of the tunes at present in vogue running too high for true congregational use.

It can hardly be expected of the average accompanist that he qualify himself to transpose long and intricate anthems, abounding in modulations, etc. This requires an expert harmonist and much routine; but to transpose such examples as have here been given requires comparatively little study.

Mode of Practice in Transposition. The proper way to begin this practice is to take keys where the notes themselves do not change—that is, where they retain the same degree of the staff. As an example, transpose a piece in E major to E flat major. The "accidentals" which may occur in the piece to be thus transposed will then be simply reversed—that is, sharps will become naturals,* naturals will become flats, and *vice versa.*

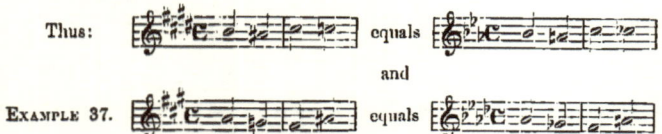

Thus: equals

and

EXAMPLE 37.   equals

Double sharps will become single sharps, and double flats single flats, and *vice versa.*

EXAMPLE 38.

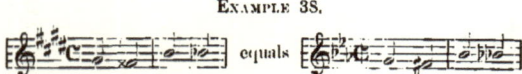

equals

Sufficient dexterity to easily command the above and similar transpositions is alone a great assistance to the voices under the conditions stated. Having conquered these thoroughly, the student may proceed to the more difficult transpositions, such as C to B, E to F ♯, etc.

Transpositions of more than a whole step will rarely, if ever, occur in Church Music.

<hr>

CHAPTER V.

ACCOMPANIMENT OF THE CHANT.

In the chant we have our simplest form of musical expression, and likewise of musical execution, as far as mere notes are concerned.

The matter becomes far from simple, however, when the player seeks to accompany the chant expressively—that is, in a manner suited to the varying sentiment of the words. By this is not meant a continual change of registration as a means of musical display, but the production of such variety as may truly aid in developing an intelligent rendering of the text. A long canticle is frequently sung to a very simple form of notes, involving the repetition of the same perhaps a dozen times or more. As the character of the words usually changes more or less during this time, it would seem that nothing would be more natural than to vary the accompaniment to suit. Such is not the case, however, with the majority of players. On the contrary, the average organist is more apt to increase the monotony of the musical repetition above alluded to than to aid in concealing it. To mitigate this monotony is certainly an important part of the organist's mission in chant accompaniment.

We can only explain this tolerated monotony, often met with among players of sufficient execution and considerable taste in other forms of accompaniment, upon the following hypothesis.

The music is indeed simple, but the ever-varying adaptation of the words to it requires an absorbing attention on the part of the player. Thus such accompanists are tied down to the notes to about the same extent as the beginner who is uncertain of the notes themselves, except by giving them the closest attention.

To get rid of this hindrance, only one cure is possible. The organist must so nearly know the words by heart as to feel himself sufficiently at ease to vary the accompaniment as desired.

This is not difficult in the ordinary canticles (having the Episcopal service in mind), but if the entire "Psalter for the Day" is chanted, it would imply a good deal of labor. Yet the case of chanting the Psalter is precisely the one where a varied accompaniment is most desirable, on account of the length and variety of the individual psalms. An actual committing to memory is not necessary, but a thorough familiarity is absolutely indispensable, at least in case of the ordinary canticles.

The organist, being then familiar with the words, is at liberty to apply to their proper rendering, and to the support of the voices, any of the means of accompaniment given in the preceding chapters. We thus avoid giving more than a few musical examples under the present head.

The two constituent parts which make up a chant are the "recitative notes" and the "spoken tones."*

EXAMPLE 39.

O come, let us sing un - to   the   Lord ;   Let us heartily rejoice in the strength of   our   sal - vation.

The first and fourth measures of the above example illustrate the former, and the remaining measures (especially those containing half-notes) the latter.

Faults in Chanting. The faults most frequently met with in chanting are two in number : 1. Attempting to *sing* the chant. In a certain sense, chanting is not singing at all, but reading to given tones. 2. Hurrying the recitative and retarding the "spoken" (half) notes. Good chanting will always invert this mode of procedure, at least measurably. The recitative tone, with its comparatively long sentence, should not be hurried beyond the time a good reader would give it in reading promptly, and with no attempts at factitious declamation. On the other hand, no choir will easily fall into the fault of giving the "spoken" tones too rapidly. Except in our best choirs, under competent leadership, these spoken tones are almost invariably taken too slow.

When and where the Organist may assist a proper performance. The nature of this work precludes the idea of here introducing a treatise on the nature of the chant, and the manner of its performance as a vocal work. It will, however, be noticed from the above remarks that during the performance of the recitative (see Example 39, Measures 1 and 4), it is impossible for the accompanist to assist the voices as to precision of utterance. He can support the intonation and the legato effect, nothing more. The case is quite different at the "spoken" tones. Here the organist can not only greatly assist the onward progress of the chant by a prompt and energetic manner of playing, but if the singers become unsteady at any period during the performance of the canticle, these are the points where he may be able to restore them to unity among themselves and the true tempo.

We give one more example covering this point.

EXAMPLE 40.

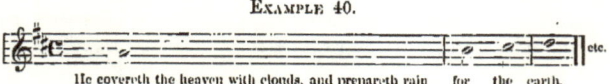

He covereth the heaven with clouds, and prepareth rain   for   the   earth.

It is evident at a glance that while the choir recite the words, "He covereth the heaven," etc., the organist can simply sustain the chord. No repetitions of the same with the voices could help the singers, or aid in steadying them. At the words, "for the earth," the organist can, however, control rhythm and accentuation to a good degree.

Steadying effect of pedal entrance. In cases of unsteadiness, the entrance of the pedals upon the "spoken" tones (premising that the pedals have not been used during the previous recitative) is one of the best means of

---

* In the Gregorian tones, so called, we have also the "*intonation,*" consisting of two tones prefixed to the first recitative. Among various works treating of these ancient melodies, the student will find one easily accessible with most excellent examples—namely, the Episcopal Hymnal, edited by the Rev. Dr. J. I. Tucker, where will be found a short, succinct explanation of the Gregorian Chant, and its manner of performance.

restoring or securing unity of performance. For this reason, among others, the pedals should occasionally be kept in reserve. In this connection, what has been said of "pedal abuse" (see Chapter IV., Example 25, Note *b*) is particularly applicable if the choir is not large. It has been seen that, in accompanying voices, the eight-foot tone must prevail as being in unison with the voices. If greater brilliancy is required, the four-foot stops are next added. Only in case of a chorus is the sixteen-foot tone to be added to the manual in chords, unless possibly in accompanying a quartet, when the four voices sing in unison. In the chant, it is sometimes advisable to double the intervals of the chord as written. This should only be continued for a measure or two, and the effect of thus filling up the chord in the left hand will be that of drawing a stop of sixteen feet equal in power to the original combination. Thus the sixteen-foot effect is temporarily produced by the fingers without drawing a stop, and will emphasize the words when fittingly employed.

Doubling the Intervals of a chord, instead of adding Stops of Sixteen-foot tone.

EXAMPLE 41.

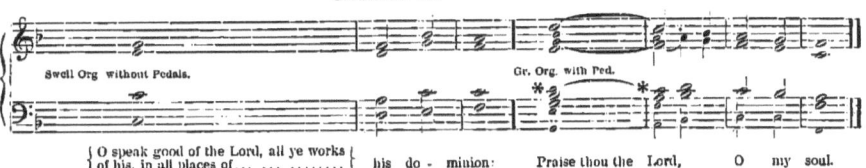

{ O speak good of the Lord, all ye works }
{ of his, in all places of... ... . }   his do - minion·   Praise thou the Lord,   O   my soul.

Example 41 represents the latter half of a Double Chant. The first three measures are accompanied upon the Swell or Choir Organ. At the fourth measure, the Great Organ enters with pedals, and the chords "filled out" during the words, "Praise thou the Lord." With the words, "O my soul," the pure four parts are resumed.* The small notes represent the tones added by the player, the large notes the vocal parts. The additions to the left hand produce the sixteen-foot effect. Those to the right hand simply aid the fulness and balance the left.

If the chord had chanced to lie lower in the left hand, the sixteen-foot effect would have been still more perceptible.

It is evident that "consecutive octaves" abound in such cases, but so they do whenever stops of different pitch are added to an eight-foot combination, and the fingers execute but four strict parts. When, however, the four parts are themselves correct, the effect of such additions is simply that of strengthening or enriching the harmony In Example 41, "consecutive fifths" may also seem to occur between measures 4 and 5 in both hands. Careful examination will show

Apparent "consecutive octaves and fifths."

that the progression is not really [♪♪♪] but thus: [♪♪♪] We here

extract the following from Hopkins' excellent work upon the organ (see second note, Chapter I., page 7) as bearing upon the preceding matter:

"The organ should be used in a somewhat different manner when any sixteen-foot manual stops are drawn, otherwise the excellent effects which that class of stops are especially calculated to produce will be to some extent obscured. The omission of all 'Doubles,' as a rule, from the

Of adding the Sixteen-ft. Manual Stops.

---

* Doublings of this kind should rarely, if ever, occur on the "spoken" tones, except as a resolution of the preceding recitative chord as above. Employed on the spoken tones, such treatment would tend to obscure the harmony.

manuals of English organs, until of late years, rendered it compulsory on organists to invent a sort of substitute for them *in effect;* for it was found that the organ-tone lacked the requisite gravity and dignity, however numerous the unison-stops might be. Performers on that instrument, therefore, had to lay aside the purer and more strict style of playing, as being ' ineffective,' and to fall back upon the system of keeping some eight or nine notes down at a time, to draw from their instruments any thing approaching a broad and massive character of tone.

"Latterly,* the serious omission above adverted to has been supplied, by addition to old organs, and by incorporation in new ones. The care already hinted at, as being required in playing on an instrument possessing so valuable an acquisition, consists in not adopting so full a style of playing when the sixteen-foot stops are drawn as when they are not. The former is viewed as rather a complicated *substitute* for the latter ; and if *both* are had recourse to simultaneously, the one is most likely to destroy the effect of the other. A very charming contrast may, however, frequently be produced in accompanying a chant or choral, sometimes in four parts *with* the Doubles drawn, sometimes in about six *without* them."

Difference between drawing a " Double " Diapason and doubling the Chord.

While these remarks are very true, it must be understood that the author has the English choirs in mind, which are largely composed of boy Sopranos and Altos. To our, comparatively few, large chorus choirs of mixed voices, these remarks would also apply. The voices of boys, from their peculiarly penetrating quality, and, moreover, from the fact that they are strong just where the female compass is weak, require a fuller accompaniment than the same number of voices in a mixed chorus.

The " filling in" the chord which we have illustrated is, of course, quite a different effect from that of using a sixteen-foot stop *throughout* a whole chant, and can readily be employed when it would be inconvenient, if not impossible, to continue playing in four parts and add a " Double" for a measure or two. A *continuous* " filling in" of the chords would prove very objectionable, for it must be remembered that *all* the stops drawn give the added tones ; while in case of a " Double" added to an eight- and four-foot combination, this stop *alone* gives the lower octave, and has been voiced by the organ-builder (that is, if he has done his duty) to blend in this connection.

Support during the " Recitative."

Where many words occur upon the recitative tone (as in Example 41, " O speak good of the Lord," etc.), it is sometimes useful to give the voices additional support towards the close, especially if the sentence be subdivided by one or more commas, as in this instance. This may be accomplished by the reservation and re-entrance of the pedals as previously mentioned. In this instance, we wish to reserve the pedals for the culminating phrase, " Praise thou the Lord !" The additional support may be given thus :

EXAMPLE 42.

The recitative is here given in $\frac{3}{2}$ measure, in order to represent, as nearly as possible, the equal division of the sentence recited. At "all ye works," the left hand changes to the Great Manual. At "in all places," the octave is added. In some cases, the single tone (without adding the octave) will be found sufficient for the purpose intended. It is by such apparent trifles as this that a good accompanist will often control the crescendo and diminuendo of his singers —they instinctively feeling what he desires of them. Technique on the part of the player is not so much demanded here as taste.

EXAMPLE 43.

Praise the Lord, O my soul:

This arpeggio indicates, as nearly as may be, a frequently employed form of beginning the chant. Each note of the chord is to be held down as the arpeggio rises, and the notation does not exactly indicate the manner of performance, which may be *ad libitum*. As to the speed at the beginning, it must not be so rapid but that the " building up" of the chord may be clearly distinguished. On the other hand, it must be equally removed from a sluggish, rhythmic addition of note to note. The term "upward roll" best characterizes the effect. In this connection, see Chapter III., Example 22, and the following remarks.

The Arpeggio in commencing a Chant.

The practical advantage of this mode of beginning is to help a choir to commence the first recitative promptly together. Singers soon accustom themselves to seize upon the culmination of the arpeggio as the point where the voices are to enter, and in chanting much depends upon beginning simultaneously.

The form of the arpeggio may also be varied so as to introduce passing notes. By this means, other inversions of the chord may be led to. Thus, in Example 43, the arpeggio leads to the fifth of the chord.

Other forms of the Arpeggio.

EXAMPLE 44 (LEADING TO THE THIRD).   EXAMPLE 45 (LEADING TO THE OCTAVE).

At *a*, Example 44, it should be noticed that the lower third in the bass is not held, as the arpeggio resolves itself into the chord proper. This is on account of the doubled third which occurs in the full chord. This is sufficient to balance the chord without the low *A*, which would only tend to obscure it. This also applies at *a*, Example 45.

In Example 43, the higher tone arrived at (*c*) as the culmination of the arpeggio sustains the addition of the lower tone by way of balance. Besides this, the chord thus created contains a *triple* fifth and tonic of eight-foot pitch without considering the pedal tonic of sixteen feet.

At *b*, Example 44, the octave (*F*, last note but one of the arpeggio) is not held down. This is in order that the diatonic leading of the passage to the upper third may be distinct.

At *b*, Example 45, *A* is the last note held down for the same reason.

This "upward roll" may also be introduced at other points than at the beginning of the chant. This, if employed, will generally occur at a change from Swell or Choir to the Great Organ. An illustration of this is the last measure of Example 42. In such cases, the arpeggio must be executed with greater rapidity than is usually employed at the beginning of the chant. It will also be noticed that the arpeggio leads to a doubling of the chord as spoken of under Example 41. For this reason, this form is best adapted to strong registration and words of relatively jubilant character. Expert organists sometimes add chromatic passing tones to the arpeggio. These should not be attempted unless they can be executed with absolute neatness and precision.

Ornamentation sometimes introduced.

As the double chant is divided into two equal portions, of seven measures each, each of which divisions takes in a verse in its performance, the central point between these two halves is termed the "*mediation*" of the chant. In antiphonal (responsive) singing the second half is performed by the second choir or division of voices. In chants of a slightly more elaborate character than usual, organists sometimes introduce at the mediation a slight ornamentation of the accompaniment, as it were connecting the two divisions of the chant. This may be the more appropriately introduced if the *harmonic* change between the two sections is of a decided character. To do this well, *extempore*, naturally demands an expert harmonist, otherwise it had better be omitted, or at least studied out (written down) carefully in advance. As to the choir, they must (through rehearsal or usage) not be taken by surprise, but be sufficiently accustomed to wait a moment, and—listen. If the passage is properly performed, they can easily tell when to "come in." Thus they gain a moment to breathe—no slight advantage in a long chant in case of a quartet choir, or where the canticle is not sung antiphonally—and the re-entrance of the voices gives added effect.

When best employed.

This treatment must be sparingly used; by no means at every repetition, even when found in print, as it sometimes is. It is, perhaps, best suited to the opening verse and to the "Gloria Patri." All trills and unseemly runs or flourishes should be avoided. A good example follows, taken from a (MS.) "*quadruple*" chant. The first half only is given.

EXAMPLE 46.

The execution of the passage thus introduced at the "mediation" is about equivalent to the addition of one more measure, the additional measure being performed in the time of the "spoken-tone" measures; thus: ♪ or with a slight *rallentando* at the close. The rests indicate the pause made by the voices. This passage may be played either upon the Swell, leading to the $f\!f$ of the Great Organ, or upon the Great Organ at once with the commencement of the small notes. The latter is preferable if the next phrase is to be sung in unison.

It will be seen from the preceding remarks that the proper accompaniment of the chant is to be derived from the sentiment of the words, and this to even a greater degree than in case of quartet and other tunes. While chants differ in musical character, yet their extremely simple structure gives them such a general family resemblance that we are forced to look to their varied *treatment* if we would gain the best possible effects from their performance. In this way, no part of the church service is more impressive.

The *Gregorian* chants, so-called, are usually sung in unison or in alternate unison and harmony. They require no different treatment as to manner of accompaniment from the Anglican single or double chants. When sung in unison, they, of course, admit of strong registration, and here it is permitted the organist to show his skill in varied harmonization of the unison melody. To do this properly requires more than a knowledge of the *modern* system of harmony, as these ancient melodies are founded upon the old Greek (so-called ecclesiastical) scales, which in many respects are foreign to our present system. Thus, many of our modern chromatic progressions are totally opposed to the simple and dignified nature of these venerable melodies, and, if employed, utterly destroy their characteristic effect. (See note, page 52.)

Gregorian Chants.

In chant accompaniment, especial care must be taken to preserve continuity of organ-tone throughout the whole canticle, no matter how often the player may change the registration, or pass from one manual to another. The reason of this may easily be perceived, if we allow a choir to chant several verses without accompaniment. Frequently, recurring little breaks will be noticed, produced by the punctuation, and by the singers pausing to take breath. This the organ smooths over and conceals. A momentary pause of both voices and organ (sometimes introduced in such cases as "for He cometh—for He cometh to judge the earth") is exceptional, and does not affect the general principle.

Continuity of Organ-tone.

CHAPTER VI.

ON "GIVING OUT" THE TUNE.

PLAYING over the tune before the voices begin, or "giving it out," as it is generally called, is susceptible of a great variety of treatment. In fact, it is only limited by the size of the instrument and the taste, invention, and skill of the player. We have elsewhere alluded to the simplest form for this purpose—namely: playing the tune over upon the Swell without pedals, and with a combination of greater or lesser power as the music to be rendered may require.

Solo treatment.
In this chapter, we propose to speak of but two methods of giving out the tune. Both of these will illustrate the treatment of the melody as a solo, and the obligato treatment of the pedals—the latter at least to some extent, if not strictly so employed.

In the following example (47), the voice parts are given for the purpose of comparison with the form of accompaniment given in Example 48; also the words of one verse as a key to the general sentiment.

EXAMPLE 47 (AS WRITTEN AND SUNG).

EXAMPLE 48 (AS GIVEN OUT).

Example 48.—The registration is here supposed to be nearly as follows: in the Swell, the Oboe and Stopped Diapason; in the Choir (or Great Organ, if the instrument possess but two manuals), the Dulciana or Stopped Diapason. If the Swell Cornopean or Trumpét eight feet were the Solo-stop, we should wish *both* Dulciana and Stopped Diapason as accompaniment.

In the Pedal Organ, the Bourdon sixteen feet is the only stop drawn.

At *a*, the sixteen-foot tone only will be heard.

At *b*, the Pedal to Choir (or Great) Coupler is drawn, thus giving both the sixteen- and eight-foot tone to the bass on the second beat of the measure, while the manuals enter upon the third beat. The difference between the beginning of Examples 47 and 48 should be noted. This is merely optional, but if the commencement, as in Example 47, be preferred, the first note of the melody should be played alone, the harmony entering with the first full measure.

At *c*, it will be noticed that the pedals do not follow the melodic form of the vocal bass, but descend to the lower octave. This is caused by the fact that the melody being given expressively, and as a solo upon the Swell, obliges the right foot to occupy itself with the Swell Pedal throughout the tune. Consequently, the left foot alone must execute the Bass part.* The imperfect legato which will thus arise, from the use of but one foot, is only justified on the ground that the melody *is* being treated as a solo, expressively, and *must* receive the first attention; further by the strict legato of the left hand upon the second manual. *Pedal lower octave employed.*

At *d*, comparison of Examples 47 and 48 will quickly show that the part played by the left hand, in accompanying the Swell Solo, is virtually no other than that of reproducing the *Trio-playing.*

* The technical management of the right and left foot under such circumstances will be spoken of later. See Chapter X.

Alto and Tenor parts—the Bass being allotted to the pedals. This is a species of "trio-playing," differing only from the usual acceptation of this term in organ-music proper, in that it is not written in three strict parts for the three sets of keys, one part to each—namely: two manuals and pedals. The student should carefully note *what* has been added to the Alto and Tenor parts (as given by the left hand), both by comparing our two previous examples and by trying the effect practically upon the organ. When the pedals, as here, are employed in the lower octave, such additions are useful, because they give the accompaniment a better blending harmonic quality considered independently by itself.

Continuance of Rhythmic Motion in Accompaniment.
At *e*, note the progression, in the left hand. This, it will be seen, differs considerably from the voice parts as to melodic form and progression. Its explanation is found in the peculiar effect (see Example 47) given by the motion of Alto and Tenor, alternately or together in quarter notes, in nearly every measure throughout the tune. Such motion must always be preserved in the accompaniment to the solo-stop, nor must added harmonies be allowed to obscure the progression of such motion.

When the Pedals execute the Bass "as written."
When circumstances allow us to free the right foot from the Swell Pedal in solo treatment, the Bass part should be executed by the pedals *as written*. The Alto and Tenor parts may then be usually played in their integrity by the left hand, thus giving us four pure parts, with the pedals treated *obligato*. This can always be done when the solo is played upon a string-toned stop of the Great Organ instead of reed, and accompanied upon the Choir Organ. The same is true of such a solo upon the Choir Organ, either with the Clarionet (reed) or string-toned stop accompanied upon the Swell or Great Organ.

At *f*, Example 48, the melody note need not be repeated, owing to the decided harmonic change (of chord) beneath it. Chapter II., Example 6, has already illustrated this principle in choral accompaniment.

Change of Manuals.
At *g*, both hands may pass to the Swell Organ, omitting the pedal part. This is nearly equivalent to a change of registration, and good in this case on account of the similarity existing between the first and third phrases of the tune. The change is here made to the manual which has borne the melody from the first. A change to another manual, differently registered, and for the duration of one phrase, is apt to sound too radical in pieces of such brief length, and savors of unworthy affectation. There are, however, some few exceptions to this, which a decided change in the character of the music will indicate. Such exceptions will usually suggest themselves in tunes of somewhat greater scope.

Of the use of the "Tremulant."
It may here be said that if the "Tremulant" (or "Tremolo") has been used with the Oboe in performing the first half of the tune, it is not advisable to continue it at *g*, where both hands play the full harmony upon the Swell. The effect of this mechanical appliance (the Tremulant) differs very widely among our organs. It is either *good*, when it beats quickly and promptly, or insuperably bad, when it beats slowly and hesitatingly. The Tremulant is generally abused by being used too frequently, and in passages not suited to it. If an organ possess a fair *Vox Humana*, it may be used in four-part harmony with the Tremulant drawn, and with good effect *if continued but a short time*. This is less advisable with the other reeds.

The shutting-off of the Tremulant (assuming it to have been used in Example 48) may be accomplished thus:

EXAMPLE 49.

The right hand here takes the chord upon the Swell at *a*, the pedal note being prolonged to support it. Simultaneously with this, the Tremulant is shut off by the left hand, which is thus made free. The slight break which the phrase permits at the double bar also aids to make this change easy.

Both hands unite upon the Swell (now without Tremulant) at *b*.

The Tremulant, thus shut off, had better not be resumed again during the remainder of the tune with the entrance of the voices so speedily approaching.

At *h*, Example 48, the solo treatment is resumed, the left hand returning to the Choir (or Great) Organ.

Before leaving this example, we would call attention to the fact that none of the tones given by the solo-stop, in Example 48, are found *in actual unison* with the same tones in the accompaniment. This individualizes the effect of the solo-stop, especially if it be a reed, and the student should endeavor always to treat his accompaniments to a given solo-stop in this manner. *(margin: Unisons between Solo-stop and Accompaniment.)*

The above is doubly true when the Tremulant is employed, as the "shaking tone" and the firm organ tone mutually injure each other if they thus meet.

The change from "giving out" the tune to accompanying it may, in case of Example 48, be made thus : *(margin: Change of Registration after " giving out " the Tune.)*

EXAMPLE 50.

At the first quarter rest (*) the reed is shut off, leaving, for the moment, the Stopped Diapason only. At the second rest, another stop is added to the Swell (but not a reed), and the pedals may be coupled with the Swell ; the pedal tone, which consists of the Bourdon, sixteen feet, coupled to the Choir, meantime continuing.

In reference to the solo upon the Swell, it is evident that the accompaniment upon the Choir or Great Organ can not follow the different shades of expression given by the solo-stop. In other words, the Choir or Great Organ can not increase or diminish the power of a set combination. For this reason a relatively weak power should be employed, which may be somewhat too weak to well support the Swell crescendo when at its height. On the other hand, it has at least this advantage, that it will not be too loud when the Swell is used in diminuendo. Much depends upon the player's skill in management of the Swell in such case. *(margin: Balance of Accompaniment to a Swell Solo-stop.)*

EXAMPLE 51.

This example, like No. 47, gives the voice parts for the purpose of comparison with the following Example 52. It furthermore gives certain *ornamentation* for the organ (small notes) which is not added, but belongs to the original composition, and is essential to its rhythmic flow. It will be observed that the sentiment of the hymn is that of triumphant joy. This is still more evident in the succeeding verses. This justifies the following treatment and registration:

The Solo "given out" in Tenor range.

EXAMPLE 52.

The registration is here supposed to be, Great Organ Diapasons and Trumpet of eight feet (possibly four-foot Principal or octave also); Swell Diapasons of eight feet, with reeds of eight feet; Pedal Organ, sixteen and eight feet, coupled to the Swell.

At *a*, the theme is given out in the lower octave as compared with Example 51, or at "tenor pitch." It is this which, in connection with the registration, gives it dignity, as this middle compass is full-toned and characteristic in most stops.

The accompaniment is again seen to be the reproduction of the Alto and Tenor parts (as in Example 48), with the addition of certain complementary tones to give fulness to the harmonies of the first and second measures more especially.

The new feature in Example 52 is that the accompaniment lies above the melody. On this account, stops of four feet can rarely be added to the Swell (with an eight-foot combination upon the Great Organ) in accompaniments of this kind, as they would extend such accompaniments another octave higher than the melody. If, however, the Great Organ combination contains a comparatively strong four-foot stop, one or two four-foot stops of mild intonation may be added to the Swell. It may be well for the student to realize the *actual effect* thus produced by the performance of Example 52 with this combination. The following represents the tones actually heard: *Accompaniment above the Melody.*

EXAMPLE 53.

etc.

The series of tones at * is obtained from the Swell four-foot stops which are coupled with the pedals.

The accompaniment lying higher than the theme, a careful use of the Swell Pedal is at times necessary to subdue the accompaniment to such a degree that the attention may not be called off from the melody proper, and unduly attracted to the melodic progression of the Swell itself. Measures 3 and 4, as far as the letter *c*, Example 52, illustrate this. For this reason the use of one foot obtains here, as in Example 48, except in case of modern instruments provided with either a "balanced" or a so-called "ratchet Swell Pedal." This will be referred to later. *Aid of the Swell Pedal in this form of Accompaniment.*

At *b*, Example 52, the figure assigned to both hands in Example 51 is given to the left hand alone. This represents the proper balance, as the melody is now played an octave lower than as given in Example 51.

At *c*, both hands pass to the Swell Organ to represent by diminished power the relation of the solo voice to the remainder of the tune.* (See Example 51.)

At *d*, attention is called to the slightly varying harmonization as compared with Example 51. This is simply a matter of convenience to the fingers, while the variety produced by inversion of the harmony can only be desirable.

At *e*, the passage in sixteenth notes may be taken at once upon the Great Organ, thus becoming an integral part of the melody proper. It may also be played upon the Swell, if preferred, in which case it must be executed with the left hand.

---

* In the performance of this tune the Solo is usually given alternately to a Soprano and Tenor voice ; but in the last verse, at the words, "Hail the Sun of Righteousness !" *all* the voices unite upon the melody. In this case the accompaniment continues upon the Great Organ, with perhaps *increased* registration.

At *f*, during the hold ⌢ upon the pedal, the Great Organ reed is shut off, other stops added if necessary, the Great to Pedal Coupler drawn, and the accompaniment of the voices begins.

Harmonic difficulties arising from inversion. This form of "giving out the tune"—in the Tenor range—requires some care in consequence of the inversions of the harmony which arise. Experienced harmonists will at once perceive that by this process a sequence of fourths (allowed in composition) becomes, by inversion, a sequence of fifths, which is justly forbidden. For the benefit of those to whom this may not be clear an illustration follows.

EXAMPLE 54. (MELODY IN SOPRANO: EXAMPLE 55. (MELODY IN TENOR:
HIGHER THAN ACCOMPANIMENT.)   ACCOMPANIMENT ABOVE.)

At the asterisks (**), Example 54, the sequence of fourths will be noticed occurring between the Alto and Soprano. In Example 55, these fourths have, by inversion, become fifths occurring between Tenor and Soprano.

A possible correction of Example 55, by beginning with the third of the chord as the highest note of the accompaniment, and thus restoring the sequence of fourths, would be the following:

Inversion, when to be avoided.

EXAMPLE 56.

The effect of this is rather artificial, and where a prolonged sequence occurs it will generally be advisable not to attempt its inversion. Where the inversion will only produce an occasional fifth progression—not a sequence of them—it will be found easy to avoid the same.

This form is also particularly well suited to many plain choral tunes. We give below the familiar old " Dundee" in this treatment:

EXAMPLE 57.

(or 8va lower)...

Here no "expressive" use of the Swell is required. It may remain open, the registration being properly balanced with the Great Organ, and both feet used for the pedals.

The only explanation required by the above example applies to the contrapuntal figuration of the second and fourth strains. This figuration of the accompaniment is not obligatory. The simple inversion in half notes might have been given. It, however, adds harmonic interest to the accompaniment, and forms an excellent exercise for those who are pursuing theoretical studies in connection with organ lessons, as they can use such exercises practically when written out. Only a tolerably expert harmonist should attempt this form *extempore*. In case this is done (*extempore*) in giving out the tune with the ordinary setting of the same before one's eyes (that is, with the *Cantus-Firmus* in the Soprano), it is frequently easier to play it as follows, without the previously given figuration of the accompaniment : *Contrapuntal Figuration.*

EXAMPLE 58.

In this way, although the position of the *Cantus-Firmus* may render the execution a little awkward, yet the *mental operation* (that of inverting the melody) is assisted ; for the right hand now executes the melody, in so far fulfilling its usual task, while the player reads it as Soprano from the book containing the tune, but plays it, as it stands, an octave lower. *Another form of Inversion.*

It will be noted that the introduction of the quarter-note motion (see second strain of Example 57) requires the employment of the same motion in the co-related fourth strain. This on grounds of symmetry. Had we *begun* the tune with this motion, it would have been necessary to have continued it throughout. *Continuance of Motion.*

But one form of greater elaboration remains to be considered among the various modes of giving out tunes as solos. This is the so-called Choral Prelude, of which Bach has given us so many admirable specimens, some of extended length. These are unsuited to our church use for two reasons: First, the service of the Lutheran Church, for which Bach wrote, begins with the singing of a choral. Therefore, extended compositions, based upon the first choral for the day, could form the "opening voluntary" or organ prelude. This was logically succeeded by the choral itself sung by choir and congregation. Second, most of these chorals upon which Bach founded his preludes are but little known (unfortunately, for they are the finest extant) and rarely used in this country at present. An example of what our ordinary services might permit follows. The figuration is probably as elaborate as would be found suited to actual church *Choral Preludes.*

use, although a richer figuration and more extended development furnish excellent organ study, both theoretical and practical.

Advanced students will find it an interesting and profitable task to construct forms of giving out the tune similar to the following. The choral melody (*Cantus-Firmus*) may be placed in either Soprano or Tenor, and even in the Bass. In this latter case the Pedal is usually registered with four-foot tone.

The tune "Mear" forms the subject of the following treatment. It will be understood that the Swell is not used expressively, as the nature of the tune does not require it, and the pedals require the use of both feet.

EXAMPLE 59.

In Example 59, the four preludial measures previous to the entrance of the *Cantus-Firmus* establish the contrapuntal motion which is to continue throughout, and the essential *motive* of the same may be thematically employed throughout in this kind of treatment.

In such forms, care should be taken so to construct the bass, by means of deceptive cadences, suspensions, etc., that the tune may have everywhere a continuous contrapuntal flow, and not divide itself into the too evident four sections corresponding with the four-line stanza. See in illustration of this the avoidance of the chord of G in accompanying the first two notes of the *Cantus-Firmus;* likewise the avoidance of the cadence at measure 9. Furthermore, measures 9 and 10, also 13–14 and 18–19, will show the manner of treating the pause ⌒ occurring at the conclusion of each strain in the original.

Avoidance of Cadences.

If choral preludes are developed at considerably greater length than Example 59, they may be appropriately used for voluntaries; more especially at the conclusion of a service where the tune upon which they may chance to be founded has been previously sung. The choral preludes of Bach furnish an inexhaustible store of models to the organ student who would try his hand at this species of composition.

In many instances, precisely the opposite treatment (as compared with the use of these forms for *actual preludes*) might find greater favor. This is the *curtailment* of tunes in giving them out. Thus, when a familiar tune is to be sung congregationally, it will often suffice for the organist to give out but a portion of it. A few measures only will inform the congregation as to the tune proposed for the given hymn. The organist can readily introduce a simple cadence, bringing the prelude to an early close, so soon as (in his judgment) the tune has been recognized.

Curtailment in giving out Tunes.

This mode of procedure is particularly advisable when hymns containing verses of six or eight long lines are announced, necessitating " double tunes."

CHAPTER VII.

ACCOMPANIMENT OF SOLO VOICES.

Peculiar diffi-cultics. Thɪs subject is one of the most difficult to treat satisfactorily, with pen and ink, of all the varied forms included under the general title of this work.

In the preceding chapters, we have had to contend principally with the fact that organs differ, and with the difficulty of deducing from the examples cited such general principles as might prove of every-day use. We are now still further limited by the fact that individual voices differ in even a more marked degree than the instruments.

For this reason, we shall be obliged to content ourselves with such hints only as may be generally made useful, applied to any instrument and any voice, leaving to the student their application to particular cases.

In the Preliminary Remarks, the nature of good accompaniment was defined as that which gives the soloist a sense of *support* upon the one hand, and of *freedom* upon the other. It will, then, be necessary to see by what means the player may aid in securing these two important requisites.

Repetition of the Melody in the Accompaniment. In ordinary accompaniments, more especially in such as have not been expressly prepared for the organ by one who understood his business, we frequently find the melody, as sung by the vocalist, continuously repeated in the accompaniment.

Now, in orchestral accompaniment—both in opera and oratorio—nothing is more common than for the first violins to move in unison with the solo voice for a while, and this even in comparatively florid passages. This, however, is justified in several ways. *First.* By the peculiarly blending quality of stringed instruments, well played, with voices of all kinds. *Second.* By the ability of good string-players to instantly follow all gradations of light and shade to a much more complete degree than the wind instruments, among which, in the present case, the organ is to be classified. *Third.* The orchestra has a conductor, while at the organ the player ordinarily sits with his back turned to the singers.

Method some-times employ-ed to indicate Accompani-ment. In some of our church music books, where the tune or anthem is printed upon four staves, without a special part assigned to the accompaniment, we find frequent illustrations of the repetition of the melody as spoken of. Indeed, in case of a Soprano Solo, the notes of the solo are usually continued of the *same size*, while small notes are introduced beneath it to represent the completion of the accompaniment. If the small notes alone are played, the harmony will not unfrequently be found "empty," without some notes of the melody to complete it. The voice, singing at the same time with the small notes played as accompaniment, does not seem to atone for this emptiness, but the accompaniment to desire its own independent (harmonic) completeness. So the average accompanist plays the melody with the voice as in the following example:

EXAMPLE 60.

Praise Him with song ex - ult - - ant, His glo - - ry loud pro-claim, To Him, etc.

This illustration may be somewhat exaggerated; but, if so, only enables the pupil to discern more easily the point at issue. Are the two conditions of support and freedom to the singer here fulfilled? That of support, possibly; but that of freedom, certainly not. In fact, the delivery of the singer is hampered by the melody being repeated by the player, while the accompanist is hampered by the attempt to render every note exactly with the singer. The slightest discrepancy would here be apparent.

Objections to this mode.

Besides this, a registration strong enough to support not only the singer's intonation, but also to characterize the sentiment of the words, would, in the majority of similar cases, have the effect of the voice accompanying the organ instead of the opposite relation. Of this sort of accompaniment, our churches already furnish too many examples.

EXAMPLE 61.

Praise Him with song ex - ult - - ant, His glo - - ry loud pro-claim, To Him, etc.

etc.

In the above example, the two middle parts (Alto and Tenor) of Example 60 are seen to have become the two upper parts of the present Example 61, with a supplementary part added below them. Thus, the harmony is complete in itself, while it will be seen at once that the voice is well supported harmonically, and yet left at perfect freedom to execute the passages assigned to it. See, in this connection, remarks under *g* and *h*, Example 25, page 31. Example 61 is supposed to represent an episodical solo in the midst of an anthem. If, then, any thing which has preceded renders the *entrance* of the solo voice uncertain, the accompaniment may be modified thus:

How to modify and improve the previous Accompaniment.

EXAMPLE 62.

The accompaniment then continues as before.

It must not be understood from the preceding remarks that three-part accompaniments may not sometimes prove of excellent effect, the solo voice representing a fourth part in the harmony. Such accompaniments require to be planned with care.

Three and two part Accompaniment.

They will generally be found written out, so as to require no adaptation on the part of the player, and are useful in producing variety of effect when preceding or succeeding a fuller accompaniment. In the example which follows, a specimen of momentary *two-part* accompaniment also occurs at the second N. B.

EXAMPLE 63.*

It is to be noted that in Example 61 the rhythmic motion is maintained by the solo voice itself. On this account, the accompaniment may well contain less motion, although, in this particular case, it will be found to possess its own rhythmic steadiness, if played alone. Where the solo voice momentarily pauses, as at the beginning of the third measure, there the motion increases in the accompaniment.

Students who possess the requisite knowledge of harmony, predicated of them in the Preliminary Remarks, will be surprised to find how little study, comparatively, will enable them to improve, modify, and adapt accompaniments according to the principle here advanced. In this way, their own task in performance will be simplified, while the soloists will receive both the support and the freedom which they desire.

Should students not possess the elementary harmonic knowledge referred to, the author can only hope that they may gain from this book such an idea of what they have yet to learn that they forthwith address themselves to the task. No one can become even a respectable accompanist without a theoretic foundation to some extent. The day is happily passing by for the phrase to be accepted: "He (or she) plays well enough to play in church."

The form of accompaniment in Example 61 may, in some respects, be termed *obligato*. It is not strictly so, in that it has no real melodic significance of its own, but simply conforms to the requirements of the solo as to harmonic support. It is, then, "*obligato*" only in the sense that it is wholly distinct from the voice part, and has its own harmonic independence without calling upon the voice to complete the same, as at Example 60.

The true obligato form will be considered under its own especial head.

We have spoken of motion in the accompaniment as contrasted with, and avoiding motion which may occur in the solo voice. We now give a good example of both of these points, together with an illustration of a case where the accompaniment may appropriately move in unison with the voice.

Margin notes: Relative motion between Voice and Accompaniment. — Apparent "obligato." — Unison of the Voice and Accompaniment.

---

* "*Dies Iræ.*" Special Hymns in Anthem form, D. B.—G. Schirmer, New York.

EXAMPLE 64.*

HENRY WILSON.

At *a*, the first two measures establish the quarter-note motion which is to prevail throughout the solo.

At *b*, the entrance of the solo voice with this motion renders it possible to dispense with the same in the accompaniment for a measure or two. Were this lack of motion to continue too long, the rhythmic accent would suffer, as the progression of the voice alone would not atone for continued lack of motion in the accompaniment. For the time being, however, the solo voice is by this means thrown into strong relief against the accompaniment, which is of course subdued.

Conditions under which Motion in Accompaniment may cease.

At *c*, note how the composer has avoided any attempt to follow the actual voice progression at the words, "the water-brooks," thus giving the soloist freedom of execution and expression.

At *d*, the accompaniment follows the solo voice, repeating the melody in unison. This may be explained as follows: The quarter-note motion prevails here *in all the parts*, but with constantly shifting harmonies. The regularity of the rhythm is such that it requires little care to insure perfect unity of progression between the singer and accompanist. This being secured, the repetition of the melody in the accompaniment is welcome, especially in supporting the crescendo, "So longeth my soul," etc. It is thus seen that, under proper conditions, the repetition of the melody in the accompaniment is not only justifiable, but better than any *obligato* form could be to fulfil the end desired. Under other conditions, it is equally evident that it is unadvisable, acting as a source of embarrassment to both singer and player. Experience, and the study of good compositions where the solo accompaniments are written out, can alone give the student surety in selecting the *form* of his own accompaniments—that is, where the composition is so written as to leave the *form* to his option; or, again, should he wish to write accompaniments to compositions of his own.

One field for the practical application of the principles here involved will be found under

---

* Six Short Anthems (No. 2). G. D. Russell & Co., Boston, Mass.

the head of adaptations to the organ of accompaniments originally written for the piano or orchestra. This will also be subsequently considered.

The next characteristic trait of solo accompaniment to which we would call attention is this: that *voices of low pitch bear* (or are suited with) *a higher form of accompaniment, and higher registration than those of high pitch*, and *vice versa*.

Or, expressed in other words: the accompaniment to a rather high Soprano Solo should, in the main, *underlie* that solo as to the written notes of the accompaniment, *unless* the accompaniment reproduces the melody. The same holds good of the registration, which, with the same exception, should be confined to stops of eight feet.

On the contrary, in case of Bass or Alto Solos, the notes of the accompaniment may frequently *overlie* the solo voice, and the registration may include stops of four feet.

In speaking of an accompaniment over- or under-lying the voice, its relation to the pitch of that voice is meant.

EXAMPLE 65.   EXAMPLE 66.

Thus, in Example 65, the highest tones of the accompaniment are lower than the lowest tones of the voice.

In Example 66, the accompaniment is seen to lie above the voice. In the following illustration, we have an accompaniment suited to either a Soprano or Bass Solo, according to the registration.

EXAMPLE 67.*

* Buck's Second Motet Collection, page 37. O. Ditson & Co., Boston.

It will be perceived that, if the Soprano Solo is used, the above accompaniment underlies the voice; if the Bass Solo, that it overlies it. If a practical test is made with the two solos and organ (and practical tests can alone instruct the pupil in cases of this kind), it will be found that a *mezzo-forte* combination with four-foot stops agrees with the Bass rather than with the Soprano Solo* The somewhat sombre or ponderous quality of the Bass voice may partly account for this, the "brightness" of the four-foot stops materially counterbalancing such quality in the voice. Over- and under-lying Accompaniment.

In further illustration of this principle, very many examples might be cited, but we will refer the pupil to two only, both from Mendelssohn's "Elijah." The piano edition is the composer's own arrangement from the orchestral score, and, being readily accessible, we refrain from quoting at length. The illustrations referred to are (1) the great air, "Hear ye, Israel!" for Soprano, and (2) that for Bass, "Is not his word like a fire?" Illustrations from Mendelssohn's "Elijah."

In the first case, the student will find admirable specimens of the "underlying" accompaniment. Especially is it useful to note when and where Mendelssohn has supported the voice in unison; also how he has avoided the same when the singer's freedom of delivery would be impeded by so doing. In the second air, we have an equally good illustration of the "overlying" accompaniment.

As a matter of course, the low range of the Bass voice (actual pitch) may be said to force the accompaniment to lie above it in the majority of instances. The point to which we desire to call attention, however, is this: *how much* higher the accompaniment may lie in such cases than would be supposed without giving the subject due consideration. In organ accompaniments, this is accomplished principally through four-foot registration, and not by writing or playing the notes at an undue distance from the solo voice.

In ordinary solo accompaniment, the use of reed-stops is to be avoided as a rule. When a female voice is to be accompanied, and when the accompaniment at the same time *moves with the voice in unison*, there should be no exception to this rule, as the effect is bad even when the reed-stop itself is excellent. In fact, the more characteristic the reed-stop may be in quality, the worse will be the effect. Use and Avoidance of Reed-stops.

* The real test is for the student to hear the effect of voices and organ at a distance from the keys. To this end he might get some friend to play the accompaniment, but he himself dictate the stops to be employed. This applies especially in judging the effect of the four-foot stops, which are often deceptive (particularly in the Swell Organ) as regards their "telling" qualities.

This very characteristic, however, renders the reed tone most valuable in case of *obligato* accompaniment, where its peculiar quality is employed to illustrate an independent part. (See Chapter VIII.)

Exception sometimes admissible.

An apparent exception to the avoidance of reed tone may be found in a certain class of (generally old) organs, unfortunately too frequently met with throughout the country. These instruments utterly lack "*characteristic voicing*"—that is, the stops to which such names as Oboe (Hautboy), Clarionet, Trumpet, etc., are given, are usually nearly destitute of any quality fairly imitative of the respective orchestral instruments from which they derive their names. These remarks apply for the moment to reeds only. Characteristic voicing is of comparatively recent date in this country, and by no means common to every builder as yet. If, then, the reed has no marked character *as a reed*, it may not unfrequently be employed in accompanying a female solo voice, and for the following reason.

In such organs, the voicing of the remaining stops (Flutes, at least by contrast, sometimes excepted) is very apt to follow suit and lack decided character. Such reeds, then, will sometimes add a certain feeble pungency of their own to the accompaniment (providing always that they be in tune), which does no particular harm as a too radical contrast with the voice.

In a word, if the reed lacks the essential qualities of a reed, the premises are altered, and the principle above stated can not apply.

Reeds with Male Voices.

When a Tenor or Bass Solo is to be accompanied, while the above omission of reed tone should prevail, yet here an exception may not unfrequently be allowed. This finds its justification in the quality (*timbre*) of the male voice, which assimilates with that of the reed to a much greater extent than the female voice.

EXAMPLE 68.*

EXAMPLE 69.†

* *Venite* in A, D. B., Episcopal Church Music. 2d Series. G. Schirmer, New York.
† "Sing Alleluia forth." Episcopal Church Music. 3d Series. G. D. Russell & Co., Boston.

Example 68 requires no explanation.

In Example 69, the pedal is introduced for the single note upon the entrance of the voice, in order, through its sixteen-foot tone, to give the low B flat which the manual lacks—this B flat being the starting-point of the following chromatic progression in the Bass. The re-entrance of the pedal in the third measure completes the climax desired. The registration of the Great Manual may here be comparatively strong; as, on the one hand, its chromatic progression is warranted by the monotone of the voice, and, on the other, it can not "cover" the voice, as it lies so far below it.

The avoidance or adoption of reed tone likewise applies measurably to quartet accompaniment, and is then governed by the same conditions as in case of solo accompaniment. With a chorus, the case is often reversed, even in passages sung by female voices only, as then the body of tone produced by numbers may render the pungent quality of the reed particularly desirable at times. *Reeds in Accompaniment of Quartets, Chorus, and Solos for Boys' Voices.*

In ordinary solo accompaniment of boys' voices, the reeds may be used far more freely than with female voices, on account of the mutually assimilating quality already referred to.

A form of solo accompaniment, which requires considerable experience to treat properly, is that of the Recitative. Here, the notation does not furnish a definite, but only a relative idea of the manner of performance. The duration of any given note is almost entirely optional with the vocalist. *Accompaniment of Recitatives.*

The accompanying harmonies are usually sustained softly, so as not to interfere with the distinct recitation of the singer. Sometimes, however, they take the form of short interjectional passages. In this latter case, they are usually played *forte* or *mezzo-forte*, as they then serve as interludes between the sentences declaimed, and give energy to the recitative.

EXAMPLE 70.

No. 5.   HANDEL'S "MESSIAH."

The Lord whom ye seek, shall suddenly come to his temple,   ev'n the messenger of the cov-e-nant whom ye delight in.   etc.

We have an illustration of this second form of recitative in the above example. It is seen that the voice is left practically unaccompanied. At the word "*temple*" (see third measure), the notation would indicate that the accompaniment should enter upon the second syllable of the word referred to. In such cases, this should never be done, as the entrance of the accompaniment would simply blur the close of the sentence on the part of the singer. As the singer is free as regards tempo, he can wait, in such cases, until silence again ensues. The same conditions qualify the last phrase, "whom ye delight in." *Entrance of Accompaniment after conclusion of Vocal Phrase.*

On the other hand, in the fourth measure, at the word "*covenant*," the chord should come in squarely with the voice. It will be noticed that with the beginning of the last measure a decided change of chord occurs. The accompanist must be careful in such cases not to introduce such chord too soon. The singer, having absolute freedom of delivery, may very possibly chance to prolong the tone (C) of the previous measure upon the last syllable of the word "*covenant*." On this account, the accompanist must be careful not to anticipate the proper time of entrance of the following chord. He must be equally careful not to allow a break to occur after the voice ceases.

Closing
Cadences.At the close of recitatives, it frequently occurs that two chords are appended, forming a cadence. The latter of these chords generally stands in the relation of dominant chord *to the key of the "air" which is to follow immediately.* These two chords should always be played *after the voice has concluded the phrase.*

The exigencies of confining the accompaniment to the laws and customs of notation, while the singer is left free to give his own value to the notes, sometimes leads to forms like the following from Handel's "Samson."

EXAMPLE 71.

The above furnishes us with two forms as written by Handel. The manner of performance would be nearly as follows:

EXAMPLE 72.

Harmonic
discrepancies.
Their avoid-
ance.At *a*, Example 71, measure 2, attention is called to the harmonic discrepancy between the C♯ of the accompaniment and the D of the solo voice. Also to the proper manner of performance of the same at *a*, Example 72. It will be seen that the closing cadence (above referred to) is postponed until the voice ceases. Also that this treatment involves the addition of one more measure to the original notation.

At *b*, Example 71, the student should particularly note the harmonic discrepancy at the close between voice and accompaniment; also, its avoidance at *b*, Example 72. In this latter example, the cessation of the second accompanying chord in the first measure (earlier than the notation demands) should be observed. The purpose of this is to give the voice unimpeded progress to the close. This may be done with comparative frequency where many "passing notes" occur

in the vocal cadence. As to the augmentation of apparent values in the notation (close of Example 72, *b*), the tendency of singers would be (and appropriately so) to close thus :
pure and sweet.

whereupon the organ might conclude as at the close of Example 72, *b*, or as follows, if preferred :

The scope of this chapter prevents our entering into the *reasons* which prompted the old masters to write accompaniments to their recitatives in a manner often differing from that in which they desired them performed. This part of the subject properly belongs to the analysis of the recitative as a form of composition. It suffices to call the player's attention to these differences between notation and execution ; remarking, in conclusion, that the unharmonic relation between voice and instrument, at the close of Example 71, establishes the fact that Handel expected this cadence to be played later than the mere notes would indicate.

CHAPTER VIII.

ON OBLIGATO ACCOMPANIMENT AND THE USE OF SOLO-STOPS.

Nature of the Obligato. THE characteristic trait of all obligato accompaniment to a solo voice lies in the fact that such accompaniment has a melodic significance of its own, distinct and separate from that of the voice accompanied, to which it unites itself. The effect produced is thus a compound one, and the union of the two melodies being *obligatory* (in order to produce this effect), the derivation and propriety of the term are evident.

Use of Solo-stops. As the melodic element of the accompaniment is here to be brought forward, as it were, in a strong light, it is also evident that solo-stops are particularly suited to accomplish this end. Almost any stop, Mixtures excepted, can be treated as a solo under proper conditions. It becomes necessary, then, to examine into these conditions, so as to obtain an intelligent idea of when and where a given stop may be used in obligato treatment.

Form of Accompaniment. In accompaniments of this class, it is evident that the player can not determine the *form* of them himself, as was often the case both with the plain choral tunes and those of more elaborate harmonic structure. He will find these accompaniments written out for him as they are intended to be played, and must confine himself to the notes as written. It thus becomes principally a matter of judgment as to the registration suited to bring out the independent melodic character of the obligato accompaniment. A possible exception to the player's being strictly confined to the form given might be the following. Where the accompaniment is of simple harmonic structure, a passage is sometimes singled out, and by contrasting (prominent) registration of one of its parts, say Alto or Tenor, a *quasi* obligato character is given to it, although not coming under the strict definition of the word, as it will not have any independent melodic significance.

As a matter of course, the solo treatment requisite to produce the obligato *effect* implies the use of two manuals in the majority of instances.

Avoidance of Reed tone. In the preceding chapter, the fact was noted that in solo accompaniment (more especially with female voices), *reed tone used in chords* was to be avoided. This was on account of the too radical character of these stops, not necessarily through their *power*, but through their *quality* of tone. A simple harmonic accompaniment in chords rarely requires any decided "tone color," but is usually all the better when serving as a neutral tint upon which the solo voice rests for its foundation, and through which its own characteristic quality is thrown into the foreground.

These premises are altered, and the case becomes quite different when the accompaniment contains a melody of its own, which shall at the same time contrast and unite with the solo voice. The reeds of the Swell and Choir Organ then become of the utmost value in developing such a melody, for now their duty becomes that of contrast in quality with the voice, as well as that of harmonic agreement with it. Their characteristic quality is sure to assert itself under such conditions—that is, when they have a melody of their own to enunciate. This quality brings with it the double advantage that we do not need to have the obligato part registered of a disproportionate strength as compared with the voice. It is the quality, not the power, which makes the obligato, thus treated, easily recognizable by the ear, while it still retains its proper subordination as accompaniment to the solo voice.

Application of Reed tone.

Quality versus Power.

While we have used the word "melody" above as characteristic of the obligato, yet no melody is thereby to be understood as of equal importance with the solo voice. Contrapuntal motion against the solo voice is the main characteristic, or even harmonic motion, if it be not prolonged, and does not degenerate into commonplace arpeggios.

The following examples will illustrate the use of the various qualities of organ tone—reed, flute, diapason, and string—as employed in the obligato form :

EXAMPLE 73

* *Benedic Anima* in B flat. D. B., Episcopal Church Music, 1st Series. G. Schirmer.

Example 73.—In this example of Soprano solo accompaniment, the $\frac{9}{8}$ motion (three triplets) is established in the first measure by the left hand upon the Choir (or Great) Organ. With the second measure, the reed enters, imitating the voice, not as to intervals, but in its rhythmic design, thus :

Clearness of Effect.   The voice pausing upon the high *F* of the second measure permits the ear to clearly distinguish and appreciate this entrance of the obligato, while the quality of the reed, and the interval between it and the voice, precludes the necessity of a loud registration. This obligato use of any solo-stop in accompaniment naturally necessitates the obligato treatment of the pedals likewise, unless the obligato melody is found in the Bass itself, which is then sometimes given at eight-foot pitch upon the manuals. Thus, while the two melodies are united, the obligato does not lose its character as an accompaniment, although preserving its own independent flow.

Reed tone below the Female Voice.   It is to be noted, as a characteristic of this treatment, that the reed never comes into unison with the voice, except as a passing note; furthermore, that it should, with rare exceptions, remain *below the female voice* to produce a good effect. If it lies above, it is sure to obscure it. Measures 4 and 5 of this example show how the reed may occasionally leave this range for a moment to return at once to its subordinate position. As a matter of course, the Swell Pedal must be used to preserve everywhere the proper balance of power in respect to the voice.

"Swell with Reed."   It may here be said that the expression, "Swell *with* reed" denotes that some other stop or stops are also drawn upon that manual *besides the reed.* These would ordinarily be (1) the Stopped Diapason, to add "body" to the reed, and (2) a delicate four-foot Flute. This latter rarely, especially with female voices. A soft eight-foot string tone (Salicional) also unites well with the Swell-reed, but does not add "body," but rather additional pungency. On the contrary, in organs where the reeds are excellent, as we now often find them in modern instruments, it is frequently better to let the reed speak for itself, entirely unsupported by other stops.

Relation of Reed to its own Accompaniment.   It should also be observed in the previous example that the reed *never comes into unison with its own accompaniment* upon the Choir or Great Organ. This aids in giving the obligato its maximum prominence, through its quality, and the reed always sounds better when so treated. This may, indeed, be considered a general rule in reed solos *lying above their accompaniment.* (See also remarks under Example 48, at *h,* page 61.)

Reed above the Male Voice.   In case of Tenor or Bass Solos, however, the reed may not unfrequently lie above the voice, providing that the compass be not so extreme as to hazard the blending of voice and obligato. The following excellent example illustrates this manner of treatment, and, at the same time, marks the extreme upward limit within which the reed is effective.

EXAMPLE 74.*

* *Bonum est,* in E flat, by S. P. Warren. G. Schirmer, New York.

ear - ly in the morn - - - - ing.

The fact that the male voice more readily assimilates with the reed than the female voice, would also permit the above registration to be reversed—that is, the left hand upon the Swell with reed (Swell closed), and the right upon the Choir or Great Organ, with Flute of eight feet.

It not unfrequently occurs in choirs that a solo, assigned by the composer to a Tenor or Bass, is given to Soprano or Alto respectively, and *vice versa*. **Substitution of one Solo Voice for another.**

This may frequently be allowed when the accompaniment is simply harmonic. Before doing this, in case of obligato accompaniment, the relation of the obligato to the proposed change of voice should be carefully examined, for, if properly written, it has been constructed with reference to a particular kind of voice. Sometimes this can be done with impunity (advanced theoretical students will understand that it must then be constructed according to the rules of Double Counterpoint), but more frequently it is to be avoided. Thus, if Example 74 be sung by a Soprano, the third measure would give us the following relation between voice and **When to be avoided.**

obligato: Voice. The reed tone, brought thus into actual unison with

the voice, is the very thing we wish to avoid, on account of "dissimilar qualities in unison," as before explained. This unison would even be objectionable if the obligato were given to a Flute, because the two preceding measures have avoided this, and the ear expects the treatment, thus established, to be logically carried out. As it is, the *octave* existing between the Tenor voice and the obligato obviates this.

Again, the fifth and sixth measures, if sung by Soprano, would produce unpleasant consecutive octaves between the voice and the Bass of the accompaniment. As written, it is in actual unison with the Tenor voice.

The following example illustrates the use of the obligato (with reed) *underlying* the male voice, the remaining accompaniment *overlying* it: **Reed below the Male Voice.**

EXAMPLE 75.*

Tenor Solo.

He hath re - mem - bered, re - mem - bered his mer - cy, his

(Sw.)

(Ch. with Clar.)

Ped.

* *Cantate Domino* in G. D. B., Episcopal Church Music, 2d Series. G. Schirmer, New York.

mer - - cy   and truth to - ward the   house   of Is - - ra - el.

The above solo for Tenor is here given in the bass clef, that the student may not for a moment lose sight of the actual relations of the voice to the accompaniment as regards pitch. It will be found on examination that, in this instance, the right hand (Swell) and the Pedal Bass together constitute a nearly complete harmonic accompaniment to the solo voice which *lies between them*, and this without the addition of the obligato upon the Choir Organ. As compared with the previous example, this obligato is simple accompaniment without rhythmic or other imitation, but serves to give life and animation to the solo, as well as characteristic color through the reed (clarionet).

More powerful Registration. The quality of the male voice is such that, when the obligato *underlies it* (as it does for the most part in this example), the registration may be more powerful than under the conditions of the previous illustration. In fact, it may demand, in some organs and with some voices, the use of a four-foot register of mild intonation, as well as additional eight-foot tone. This will depend largely upon the strength of the reed.

Effects in the distance. We have elsewhere alluded (note, foot of page 73) to the necessity of an organist's having a mental conception of the effect of his accompaniment as heard in the body of the church. This is doubly important in case of obligato accompaniment, for the registration is very apt to be too strong.

It must not be forgotten that a tone not sung by the voice, but heard at the same moment with it, when of contrasting quality with that voice, asserts itself in a far more decided way, and at a greater distance, than a simple chord of an assimilating quality, in which chord the voice note is duplicated. To this is to be added the fact of contrapuntal or harmonic motion (as the case may be) which is assigned to the obligato; such motion always attracts the attention of the ear. Here proper registration comes into play, for the motion must not be allowed to obscure the solo voice.

Obligato of low Compass with Soprano Voice. The Soprano voice may also be treated with an obligato accompaniment of low compass, although the opportunity will hardly offer so frequently as when the reed lies nearer the voice, as in Example 73. When the low range is to be employed for the obligato, in connection with the Soprano voice, one or more harmonic parts must intervene between it and the voice, both to preserve the harmonic completeness of the accompaniment and to form a closer union with the voice. The following example illustrates this:

EXAMPLE 76.*

The accompaniment to Example 76 is essentially in three parts, with certain points treated in four parts to complete the harmony. The compass of the obligato in this illustration is virtually that which should be adopted when it is desired to employ a string-toned stop—this range—descending to about the lowest *G* of the manual—containing their most characteristic tones. No special example is needed on this point, but a few words may be said as to their use. *(margin: String-tone Obligato.)*

Modern organs generally contain at least one string-toned stop of eight feet to each manual. Upon the Great Organ, the *Gamba;* upon the Swell, the *Salicional;* and if the organ possesses three manuals, a *Violin Diapason (Geigen Principal)* or *Keraulophon* upon the Choir Organ. The Gamba of the Great Organ is ordinarily too powerful to use for an obligato solo accompaniment, even with male voices. On the other hand, the Salicional of the Swell is generally too weak for this purpose. The voicing of the Choir Organ (lying between the two) will frequently best lend itself to the obligato treatment.

In organs of but two manuals, the player must, for the above reason, dispense with the Great Gamba, except when the obligato accompanies several voices, singing either in unison or in parts. The Swell Salicional blends charmingly with the voice in simple harmonic accompaniment (in chords), and this use is to be preferred to the obligato treatment—although it might serve in passages of great delicacy.

The Violin or Violina is the title of the string-toned stop of four feet in the Swell, and is the octave to the Salicional. Its peculiar telling quality is such, that it is better not to use it in solo accompaniment, as it never blends well with the voice, especially when heard at a distance from the keys. This does not hold good when several voices are to be accompanied, nor in organ solos. In solo accompaniment, where the four-foot tone is required, a delicate four-foot Flute added to the Salicional will accommodate itself far better to the voice.

---

* "Hail to the Lord's Anointed !" D. B., Special Hymns in Anthem form. G. Schirmer, New York.

Open Diapason Eight-foot Obligato.

The Open Diapason of eight feet in our modern organs (the Great Organ Diapason is meant) will almost uniformly be too powerful for any use with solo voices in the manner of which we are now speaking. With the older instruments built some fifteen or twenty years previous to the present day (1877), it might doubtless be made use of occasionally. With a quartet or double quartet of voices, the modern full-toned Diapason can sometimes be introduced for a short passage with fine effect, if the obligato lies beneath the whole vocal harmony. If the choir be larger, other stops must of course be added. This will cover its characteristic tone measurably, but the obligato will not thereby lose its effect. A specimen of this episodical obligato use of the Open Diapason follows, taken from the "Short Requiem" of Mozart at the passage, "*Quam olim Abrahæ promisisti.*"

EXAMPLE 77.*

Thou didst prom - ise, didst prom - ise for - ev - - - - er.

Voices.

Accomp.

The entrance of the Pedal (which is coupled to the Swell) will be noticed. By this means, the left hand is enabled to leave the Great Organ for the Swell, through which the final diminuendo is accomplished.

Flute Obligato, Eight-foot.

The whole family of Flutes, in contradistinction to the reeds, almost invariably sound better when the obligato *overlies* the voice. This arises partly from the fact that the characteristic quality of this stop, as with its orchestral prototype, lies in its upward rather than its lower and medium compass. This, it will be perceived, is a radical difference as compared with both string and reed stops.

Among the Flutes, we class the various Stopped Diapasons of wood and metal as coming essentially under this head. The fact remains, however, that an "open" Flute (that is, where the pipes are *not* stopped by a wooden plug or metallic cap) is best suited to overlie the voice. Such a stop is the Melodia or Claribella of either the Great or Choir Organ.

Double and "Rohr" Flutes

Modern instruments have borrowed from Germany two admirable stops of the Flute family, formerly unknown to our organs, but now becoming common. The Doppel-Flöte (Double Flute, with two mouths, one on either side of the pipe), an "open" stop of great fulness and body of tone, and the Rohr†-Flöte, a stopped pipe of both metal and wood, and differing by a certain agreeable *hollowness* of tone from the usual Stopped Diapason. These stops are both

---

* Second Motet Collection, page 76.   O. Ditson & Co., Boston.

† "*Rohr*" signifies in German (in this connection) the hollow reed found on wet or swampy lands or near water. Hence the appropriateness of the name above given.

of eight-foot tone, although the Rohr-Flöte is frequently met with as a four-foot stop. Neither of these stops lends itself readily to obligato use; the Doppel-Flöte on account of great fulness of tone, the Rohr-Flöte on account of the hollow quality mentioned. The former may be occasionally employed, more especially with a powerful male voice. These stops reverse the ordinary flute characteristic previously spoken of, and their best tones are those of the medium and approximately low compass. *(margin: Characteristic Range.)*

The above example, with the following, shows nearly the best solo range of the " open" Flute-stop, eight feet. It will not cover the solo voice, and, indeed, if that voice be large and full, it may require the assistance of a Flute of four feet. When the eight-foot Flute is used alone, and it is desired that the obligato descend to a comparatively low compass, the accompaniment upon the other manual should, at least, partially cease, in order that the Flute be unobscured when it reaches that part of its compass where it lacks the brilliancy which elsewhere secures attention. The ending of the solo which opens with Example 78 will show this. *(margin: "Open" Flute Eight-foot Range.)*

Here it is seen that the Swell preserves the rhythm intact, but by means of the rests the downward progress of the Flute is rendered clear.

Flutes of four feet, if of delicate quality, may sometimes be used to double the solo voice in an upper octave, as in Example 80. *(margin: Flutes of four feet)*

It is evident that the tone of the Flute is here *two* octaves distant from the voice, on which account it does not "cover," and sometimes proves useful in securing accurate intonation. It is rarely suited to obligato use, as being either too piercing on the one hand, or too delicate to be effective upon the other, according to the voicing.

The eight-foot Flute sometimes moves *with the voice* an octave higher, but this stop being ordinarily found only on the Great or Choir Organ, will usually prove too loud employed in this way, if the voice have a passage of subdued character.

---

* *Cantate Domino* in G. D. B., Episcopal Church Music, 2d Series. G. Schirmer, New York.

EXAMPLE 81.

the   first...... fruits   of   them'   that   sleep.

In this example (the ending of Handel's immortal " I know that my Redeemer liveth"), Mozart* gives the melody to the Orchestral Flute an octave above the voice. It must not be forgotten, however, that the orchestral performer can subdue his tone to *pp*. On the other hand, the Great Organ or Choir Flute, of eight feet, would be unable to do this. The Swell will probably possess no eight-foot Flute (the Stopped Diapason will not answer in quality); therefore, this effect is best represented upon the organ by a Salicional (as the *piano* of the string orchestra) and a four-foot Flute, played as written, but speaking, of course, an octave higher.

It should be evident to the student, from the illustrations thus far given, that the obligato principle will find use in adaptation to the organ of accompaniments from oratorios, masses, and the like, whenever the accompaniment takes upon itself a special melodic significance.

Three Tone qualities.

In many cases, the obligato treatment will present (as in most of the examples cited) three distinct yet blending qualities to the ear—namely : (1) the solo voice, (2) the solo-stop, and (3) the harmonic accompaniment to both of these, played upon a second manual with what may be termed a *neutral quality* of tone, but supporting both the others.

Tone contrast not a necessity.

Still, obligato accompaniment does not necessarily imply contrast in registration. Cases occur when both hands may execute both the obligato proper and the accompaniment upon one manual. In such case, the registration (for a solo voice) should be without reeds.

EXAMPLE 82.†

To   thee   Che-ru-bim and Ser - a - phim con - tin - ual-ly do   cry ....

---

* The last two measures preceding the final note as given above will be found to differ in respect to the setting of the words from both Novello's and Boosey's editions. It, however, agrees with that edited by John Bishop. The form given is taken from the orchestral score with *Mozart's additional accompaniments* lately published by Peters, of Leipzig. It is evidently correct, for by the other setting false accents occur. The small notes at the close are those assigned by Mozart to the Solo Flute and Clarionet respectively.

† *Te Deum* in E flat, by S. P. Warren. G Schirmer, New York.

The previous example illustrates this, and requires no farther comment. In accompanying a full choir, this obligato form (upon one manual) is often employed, as contrasting effects in registration would evidently be thrown away when a number of voices are singing. In this same connection, when the voices move in unison, and the organ gives the supporting harmonies, the accompaniment, by somewhat of a license, is often said to be "*obligato*." In one sense it is —that is, it is *required* to establish the harmony, modulations, etc., intended by the composer, but it is not strictly obligato in the sense we have attempted to illustrate, unless its own melodic character and independence are well defined. Thus, the following example is but a specimen of simple harmonic accompaniment :

Form sometimes called Obligato.

EXAMPLE 83.

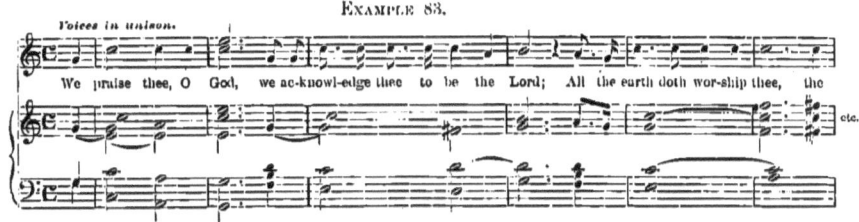

Here, it will be seen that the voices have to rely essentially upon themselves for rhythmic motion ; therefore the accompaniment, although here absolutely *necessary*, does not fulfil the idea of the true obligato. Compare with the following example :

EXAMPLE 84.*

* *Te Deum* in C. Episcopal Church Music, D. B., 3d Series. G. D. Russell & Co., Boston.

The accompaniment to Example 84 shows a melodic independence of its own, on the one hand, and on the other a greatly increased sense of rhythm.   It therefore deserves the name of obligato accompaniment, although unassisted by contrasting registration, as we have seen in accompaniment of a solo voice.   When and where the obligato form is to be preferred to the simple harmonic accompaniment is a matter for taste and experience to decide.   This of course applies to a choice in *composing* such forms.

We have previously alluded to the fact that the student can not, himself, govern the form of these accompaniments in the sense that it was found possible in choral and simple harmonic accompaniment, but must registrate them as he finds them.   Before closing this chapter, then, *Value of the* we would ask the attention of the readers of this work to a few words in advocacy of the *obligato form.* obligato form, for solo accompaniment more especially.

By way of preliminary, the author would say that he has made use of so many examples from his own church writings, against his original wish and intention, for the following reason.

. This work has been written among so many distracting professional and other duties, that it has been impossible for him to cite satisfactory specimens on this point from classical and other authorities, owing to the amount of time which the necessary research would claim, and which he reluctantly realized he could not hope to call his own.   If, however, the examples clearly illustrate the point at issue, his object—the exposition of a certain theory—will have been attained.

At the rate musical education is extending, we shall have continual accessions to the number of church composers.   It therefore behooves the young men who are studying the subject to consider theoretically the best forms of solo accompaniment, among which the obligato, although not the only one, should find a prominent place.   In the treatment which is here advocated, there is nothing essentially original as far as the obligato is concerned.   It is the principle which every organ student finds in very many compositions for organ solo, but here applied to the accompaniment of the solo voice, or even chorus.

Neither is the obligato form advocated merely for purposes of musical ornamentation, although it can produce that ; nor simply to create pleasing contrasts of tone (registration) appealing to the ear.

A source of Its real value consists in this : that it *develops and sustains* Rhythmic Motion *by means Rhythmic Mo-* *legitimate to the organ as an instrument.* *tion.*

To illustrate this important point.

Where many voices are singing together, the rhythmic accent is intensified—in case of a solo voice, it is proportionately weakened.   Here the accompaniment steps in to supply this want.   The following example is perfection itself, regarded solely from this point of view, but unfortunately it is wholly foreign to the nature of the organ.

EXAMPLE 85.

motion as is suited to the instrument ?

What, then, is to be done ?   The accompaniment here given—a common formula, suitable for piano or orchestra—is inadmissible for the organ, and yet the singer requires rhythmic assistance.   Is it not evident that we must seek it in treatment characteristic of the organ—that is, in *contrapuntal* motion more or less strict, or in such harmonic

To successfully write such accompaniments, of course presupposes the composer to have not merely a fair natural talent, but also *to have studied.* Would not a state of things which should exclude such as have *not* studied be a God-send to the Church Music of America? Study required.

The objection is often made that such accompaniments, when written, exceed the ability of the common or average organist. It must not be lost sight of, however, that the average organist of to-day is already a very different individual technically from him of even ten years ago. It must not be lost sight of that the study of the organ as an instrument is being pursued, on all sides, in a totally different spirit, and with consequent different results as compared with the manner of even ten years ago. Objection to this treatment.

The same may be said of theoretical instruction. Are we, then, to adapt ourselves to the coming generation, or to the fossils of an essentially unmusical past? To illustrate still further: let us take Example 76, and set the accompaniment as follows, premising that the rhythm has been well defined up to the entrance of the solo voice:

EXAMPLE 86.

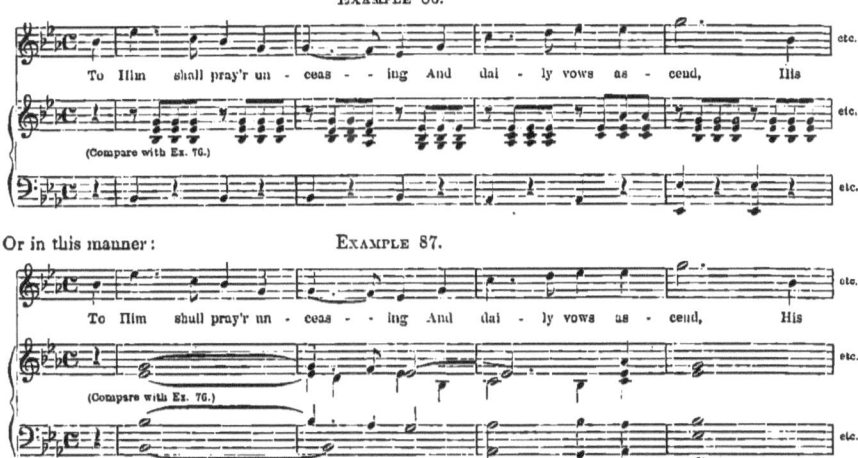

Or in this manner: EXAMPLE 87.

In Example 86, the necessary motion is indeed preserved, but with what effect as played upon the organ!

In Example 87, the organ treatment is well enough, but we lose the marked rhythm where increased, not decreased, motion is desired, and the effect suffers accordingly. Where *repose* is the effect desired, especially when the preceding movement has been brilliant, such an accompaniment (harmonic) as Example 87 furnishes may answer every purpose. Where this is not the case, but where motion *equivalent* to that of Example 86 is desired, some form of obligato treatment suggests itself at once. It is this alone which will naturally supply this motion, and at the same time be thoroughly organ-like in character. "Repose" in Accompaniment.

If these words but induce our young students, both practical and theoretical, to give this branch of the subject the special attention which the author fully believes to be its due, he will be amply repaid for his labor.

CHAPTER IX.

ADAPTATION OF PIANO AND ORCHESTRAL ACCOMPANIMENTS TO THE ORGAN.

Necessity of such adaptations.
A KNOWLEDGE of the above subject is indispensable to a good organist, for, perhaps, not one half of the compositions performed in our churches have accompaniments suitably written for the organ. Those suited only to the piano abound, even in compositions whose vocal character may render them worthy of church use. This state of things is unfortunate, for the player who may have tried the piece over upon the piano finds, upon coming to the organ, that the accompaniment falls off greatly in effect, and not unfrequently sounds simply detestable if played literally as written. Still, such pieces are expected to find their principal use in church with organ accompaniment; therefore the player has to adapt the same to his instrument as best he may. A woful amount of ignorance seems to exist as to the different ways by which an accompanist may help himself in this respect. To illustrate what may ordinarily be done to this end is the purpose of this chapter.

These piano accompaniments, thus found in works intended for almost exclusive use with the organ as accompanying instrument, have originated in one of two ways—either (1) in ignorance of how to write a proper organ accompaniment, or (2) from the fact that the original work was intended for orchestral accompaniment.

Piano Accompaniments originally so written.
As to the first, it is sometimes argued that such piano accompaniments are written that the piece may prove of use in the social circle as well as in church. The fact remains, however, that when such pieces find favor, their church use far exceeds their private use. Besides this, a very ordinary pianist can easily adapt an organ accompaniment (providing it is not *obligato*) to the piano, by repeating chords which are sustained by the organ, etc., while to adapt a piano accompaniment suitably to the organ requires much more dexterity and knowledge.

Piano Accompaniments derived from Orchestral Score.
Under the second head—namely: pieces originally composed with orchestral accompaniment—are comprised the many selections and extracts from masses, oratorios, and motets, with orchestra. The *piano* accompaniment with which these pieces are provided is but a simple reduction from the orchestral score, and the problem for the organist is to make a second adaptation fitting this derived piano accompaniment to the organ. It is in this sense only that we have to do with adaptation of orchestral accompaniments in this chapter, not with adaptation to the organ from the original orchestral score itself. This latter demands a competent knowledge of orchestration as well as of the organ, and is foreign to the purpose of this work. There are, however, occasional differences between accompaniments originally composed for the piano, and piano accompaniments reduced from an orchestral score. We shall endeavor, before closing this

chapter, to give some explanation of this, so far as it may be done without entering into the subject of orchestration proper, which is, of course, an independent study.

The first condition of accompaniment is harmonic support. Next follows the establishment of rhythmic accent. In four-part vocal work, we have already seen that the voices themselves may establish such accent, but in solos, or where voices sing in unison, this is usually insufficient. _{Contradistinction between Piano and Organ Accompaniments.}

In case of piano accompaniments, the rhythmic accent is attained by increased rhythmic motion, as compared with the vocal parts. Thus, the accompaniment may reiterate the same chord several times to one note of the voice or voices, sometimes interspersing rests to heighten the accentuation.

In organ accompaniments, on the other hand, the motion should be *harmonic* or contra-puntal rather than *purely rhythmic*, to be suited to the nature of the instrument. That this may be clearly understood, as a basis for subsequent explanation, two examples follow which illustrate respectively each kind of motion :

EXAMPLE 88.

The above illustrates a common form of *piano* accompaniment, and it is evident that the sense of motion is accomplished purely by rhythmic means, the harmonics being simple and reiterated. Played literally upon the organ as it stands, the effect would not only be wholly unsuited to the character of the instrument, but destructive to the sentiment of the text, and absolutely vulgar ! Yet how many accompaniments we find written in this manner, and played *as written*, from lack of knowledge on the part of the organist how to adapt them properly to his instrument ! In case of such an accompaniment played upon the piano, the harmonic *resonance* of that instrument seems to obviate the broken effect to a good extent, especially when the pedal is made use of, smoothing over and connecting the separate chords. Thus, a moment's thought will show that in the second measure of Example 88 (for instance), when the last chord of that measure is struck upon the piano, the two previous chords still continue sounding by means of the pedal, collecting tone, as it were, upon the same strings. With the organ, nothing of the kind occurs, and therefore the comparatively broken effect if used thus ; each chord asserting itself radically and disconnectedly. There are two ways of adapting such accompaniments, according as one or two manuals may be employed. We will first consider what may be accomplished upon one manual in the way of adaptation.

Before doing this, however, we proceed to give the accompaniment originally set to the for-mer example : _{"Harmonic" motion.}

EXAMPLE 89.*

The motion is here seen to be essentially harmonic—that is, created by *varied* harmonics rather than by reiteration of the same chords within the measure. The present treatment is not only peculiarly suited to the organ, but lends added dignity to the words—the reverse effect to that of the former example.

The momentary lack of motion in the fourth measure of the accompaniment is atoned for by the rhythmic progression of the voice at this point.

Adaptation upon one Manual. The true manner of treating such accompaniments as Example 88 would doubtless be to remodel them after the general pattern of harmonic motion as shown in Example 89. As this would be asking too much from the majority of players, we will suppose the accompaniment to Example 88 to be given, *as it stands*, for organ adaptation. The problem may be solved thus:

EXAMPLE 90.

Here, it should be noticed that the "whole notes," forming almost continuously the upper notes of the accompaniment, serve two purposes: First. They avoid the broken effect of Example 88, preserve the continuity of organ tone, and form an effective (unbroken) two-part harmony with the Bass, or a three-part harmony including the voice part. Thus, the continuity of organ tone being preserved, the "quarter-note motion" *coming between* the two extremes can not assert itself unduly, but is simply felt as a welcome addition to the rhythmic effect. If a special rhythmic accent is desired, the pedal may be employed in the first two measures as **Consonance of sustained tones. Motion below them.** represented by the small notes. Second. It should be observed that these upper tones stand continually in the relation of consonant intervals (sixths and thirds) to the voice part. In this way, an intimate harmonic relation is preserved between the voice and the sustained tones, while the repeated quarter-notes fulfil the subordinate duty of creating the desired sense of motion without disturbing the unity of the whole. That this result (Example 90) is superior to Example 88, but still inferior to Example 89, in an artistic point of view, should be sufficiently evident.

* *Te Deum* in F.   Dr. J. B. Dykes.   (Novello's Parish Choir Book—Modern Composers.)

It by no means follows, from the relation of the sustained tones to the voice (in thirds and sixths), as shown in Example 90, that other intervals may not frequently be sustained in preference to the above—such as fundamental tones (or octaves), fifths and even fourths.   To illustrate this, let us again take Example 88, and (with a few melodic alterations) *prefix the treble clef* to the voice part, thus giving us a new example :

EXAMPLE 91.

The voice now begins with the third of the chord where it originally began with the fifth. It is seen that the sustained tone is at first the fundamental tone of the chord, as also in the third and fifth measures.   The second measure is weak harmonically, in that the sustained tone creates at first a bare fourth in its relations to the voice, and a fifth to the Bass.   A more serious objection to this form is that the motion. lying exclusively above the sustained tone, renders it partially liable to the same criticism as Example 88.   A better form of treatment would be to begin with the fifth as sustained tone, thus : *Motion above the sustained tones.*

EXAMPLE 92.

At *a a*, it is seen that this accompaniment also lacks the third of the chord upon the accent of the measure.   This tone is, however, *supplied by the voice*, differing advantageously in this respect from the second measure of Example 91.

A careful comparison of these examples and the remarks applicable to each, will enable the student to deduce this general rule—namely : whatever tone is sustained, that tone must stand in the relation of a third or sixth to the voice part.   Fourths and fifths may sometimes be permitted when the effect they produce is but transient, especially when they occur upon the unaccented part of the measure.   It is to be noted further that it is preferable to have the sustained tones lie *above* the notes which give the rhythmic motion, when a reasonably legato organ effect is desired. *Application of the principle of sustained tones.*

In accompanimental figuration of a more elaborate character, the same principle will be found to obtain.   A few illustrations of the treatment of some common formulas of accompaniment follow.   From an examination of these, the pupil should be able to treat other forms as far as practicable upon the organ.

EXAMPLE 93 (AS WRITTEN).

Compare the above with the following :

EXAMPLE 94.

"Triplet" and other Figuration.

At *a*, Example 94, the triplet "springs" from the sustained tone, and the octave of the Bass (C) is "held over," so that on the last note of the triplet the full chord is heard. This corresponds measurably with the effect produced by using the pedal of the piano. It will depend somewhat upon the nature of the accompaniment desired whether these tones be held over in this manner, or the single sustained note held. For an accompaniment intended to be light and transparent, it is often preferable not to hold them, as the sustained tone will give the passage a sufficiently legato character. If the piano figure contains double notes, thus:

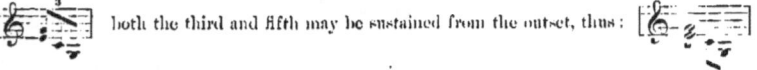

both the third and fifth may be sustained from the outset, thus:

The Manual Bass may likewise sustain the fundamental tone (as at *b*), the pedals supporting the rhythmic accent by repeating the fundamental tone.

At *b*, comparison of Examples 93 and 94 will show that by means of the eighth-rest, introduced after the first triplet has been heard, the subsequent triplets are produced by the sustained tone being heard alone on every recurrence of the rest.

At *c*, besides the form given, the two upper tones only may be held down, leaving the last two to move freely.

At *d*, three sustained tones are given in "whole notes," besides which the episodical retaining of the fifth (*g*) is to be noted in the right hand.

At *e*, Example 93, the Bass is sometimes written thus, simply for the purpose of powerfully sustaining the fundamental tone. When the piano accompaniment has been derived from an original orchestral setting, it sometimes denotes the entrance of the kettle-drums (*Timpani*). Notice that the effect at *e*, Example 94, given as an organ equivalent, is produced by a prolonged shake of the fundamental tone with the half step below ; not with the step or half step above. "Shake" or Tremolo in the Bass.

At *f*, it becomes a matter of judgment whether the "tremolo" is to be executed as given in Example 94, or by simply sustaining *all* the tones of the chord. In accompaniments of medium strength or soft effects, and even with the full Swell, especially in crescendo, such a tremolo is frequently useful. This occurs less frequently upon the Great Organ on account of the more positive quality of tone, and is to be wholly avoided when string tone predominates, on account of the slow speech of these pipes.

Examples of a similar kind to those grouped under Example 94 might be multiplied at great length, but the intelligent pupil should have no difficulty in applying the general principle of adaptation to all other forms which may be executed upon one manual. Some piano accompaniments will, of course, occur which are simply impossible to adapt with any satisfactory result as an organ accompaniment.

The employment of two manuals, while requiring a greater technical ability on the part of the performer, furnishes the means of adaptation of many accompaniments which would be found impossible adequately to adapt upon one manual. Adaptations by means of two Manuals.

EXAMPLE 95.

In the above illustrations, the sustained tones give the complete chord upon a second manual. The arpeggio, or figured accompaniment (as at *c*), is played upon the first manual—that is, upon the manual which has the strongest registration. It is evident that in this way a perfect legato is attainable, while yet the motion produced by the arpeggio is distinctly felt. This is analogous to the use of wind instruments in orchestration, which frequently sustain the fundamental harmonies while the strings move in arpeggios or other figures.

In this mode of accompaniment, the Bass must necessarily be assigned to the pedals, leaving generally a three-part chord to the left hand. This chord is, of course, derived from the arpeggio or essential harmony of the figured passage itself, therefore such a knowledge of harmony as will enable the accompanist to detect instantly of what essential harmonies such figuration is composed is an absolute necessity. The great majority of piano-forte accompaniments may, by this use of two manuals, be made available, or at least respectable, for organ use.

Subordination of the sustained Chord as to Pitch.

It will be noted that the soft chord sustained upon the second manual (Example 95, *a* and *b*) does not contain the highest note of the arpeggio given to the first manual. This method of keeping the sustained tones subordinate in pitch will be found generally advisable. With two manuals, the notes of the arpeggio should not be held down as in Example 94, where but one manual was employed. In fact, where smoothness of effect is sufficiently secured by the sustained tones of a second manual, the arpeggio may even be effectively executed with the staccato touch, care being taken to select such stops as will most promptly respond to this touch.

Registration as affected by varied Figuration.

Where the figuration is that of a simple arpeggio (as at *a* and *b* of the previous example), it is better to avoid reeds and play such arpeggios upon the Choir or Great Organ, with the accompaniment upon the Swell. For such sustained yet subdued tones, the Swell string-toned stops lend themselves with admirable effect. Flutes of eight feet are best fitted for the figuration itself under these conditions.

The case is altered to a considerable extent when the figuration ceases to be that of a simple arpeggio, and takes upon itself more of an independent melodic character as at *c*, Example 95. Figuration of this kind may appropriately be played upon the Swell with reeds, and accompanied upon the Choir or Great Organ; for here the figuration has a melodic value approaching that we have already considered under the head of " obligato accompaniment."

Alternation of Manuals.

Alternation of these effects may also be employed—that is, the figuration being alternately performed upon the Swell with reed, and upon the Choir or Great Organ without reed. Thus in the following example from Mendelssohn's " St. Paul," the accompaniment to the chorus " Happy and blest are they," is as follows :

EXAMPLE 96.

During the prelude, which opens as above, it is better to have the figuration upon the Choir Organ, that the melody which is to form the principal subject of the coming chorus may be announced upon the Swell with reed. Later, however, when the voices enter and the above is repeated as accompaniment, it is better to give the *figuration* to the Swell with reed, as the reed quality asserts itself better, and the motion will be sooner felt by the voices. The theme, which is given to the reed in the above example, being now actually sung by the voices, does not require reed registration to give it due prominence, whereas the figuration does.

Recognition of appropriate form of Adaptation.

In adapting these accompaniments, a certain expertness is requisite, in order to recognize, at sight, the *form* in which a given piano accompaniment may most appropriately assume in its organ adaptation. Thus the *original* (piano) form of Example 95 at *c* may have been expressed thus (compare with *a* of the following example):

EXAMPLE 97.

At *a*, it devolves upon the accompanist to recognize the form which he may give this purely piano-forte setting upon the organ. As it stands, it is wholly opposed to the nature of the latter instrument.

At *b*, we are led to consider certain conditions under which dissonances appear in the figura-.tion, and how they may affect the treatment of the second manual.

Dissonances frequently appear in figured accompaniments, and, if properly introduced, heighten the effect. They almost uniformly appear in the character of " passing notes," and their treatment as such is to be studied under the rules of harmony and composition. For the present, we have simply to do with the *form of harmonization with which the second manual is to accompany them*, without criticising whether the dissonances themselves are introduced in the best manner or not, but taking them as we find them. *Dissonances in the Figuration.*

For those who are unfamiliar with the general principle governing the introduction of such dissonances, it may here be said that in a figure composed of a group of four notes (as in the previous examples), not more than two tones dissonant to the accompanying chord should occur. Thus, taking the second group at *a*, Example 97, [♫] the A♭ and F♯ are seen to be the two dissonant tones, the accompanying chord being that of the dominant seventh. In the fourth group, we have three consonant tones, the F♯ alone being dissonant. In this case (Example 97, *a*), careful examination will show that the dissonant tone, whether rising or falling, leads to a *concord*, the *lowest* tone of the figuration lying *above* its accompaniment.

At *b*, Example 97, observe the progression D♯—E in the figuration, as compared with its accompaniment. The latter tone (E) is at the same time the upper tone of the second manual. It is this fact of the motion becoming *absorbed* in the accompaniment, by entering into actual unison with it immediately after the dissonance, which renders this form of the accompaniment faulty, as it produces a blurred effect or disappearance of the figuration. Should such a figuration be given, the accompanist must avoid this by an inversion of the chord. In this instance, *Faulty " absorption " of Dissonance in the accompanying Chord.*

the simplest form would be to give the left hand thus : [♫] rather than [♫]

The harmonic relation of the D♯ and E in the figuration, to the E of the accompaniment, is now changed from that of a minor second and actual unison ("*prime* ") to that of a major seventh and octave. By this means, the melodic character of the figuration is not obscured, but clearly perceived. Notwithstanding this, it will be evident that the figuration does not stand in so agreeable a relation to the accompaniment as in Example 95, *b*. This is because of the changed relation of the upper accompanimental tone to the figuration—namely, a fifth instead of a third.

Occasional omission of an Interval in in the accompanying Chord.

A full chord—that is, where fundamental, third, and fifth are represented—is not always necessary in the accompaniment; as, for instance, when the figuration is represented by  The accompaniment to this should be, [image] the two upper notes being played by the left hand, and the lowest representing the pedal tone. The reason of this is obvious when we consider both the F and D♯ in the light of passing notes (or appoggiaturas), resolving respectively from above and below to the tone E, thus forming the essential harmony.

At *c*, Example 97, we have an illustration of the treatment which may be employed when the rhythm is to be very distinctly marked. Here it devolves upon the figuration itself, with the upper tone of the accompaniment, to preserve the legato effect.

Figuration in the Bass.

When the figuration occurs in the left hand, it may, in the majority of cases, be executed as written. This is especially the case when the legato is preserved by the right hand and by a sustained pedal. A few illustrations follow.

EXAMPLE 98.

MASS IN B FLAT. NEUKOMM.

etc.

Pedal simplification. Omission of occasional Manual Notes.

The small notes at ** are added for the pedal, the original piano (or orchestral) accompaniment not containing them. This method of simplification is frequently employed in accompaniments of this kind, especially when the pedal gives, not only the fundamental harmonies, but also the vocal bass played in the lower octave as here.

It will be seen that if the above be played upon the Great Organ, *with that manual coupled to the pedal*, there will be an interference of the left hand and pedal upon the first note of each measure. On this account, it is advisable to execute such passages after the following formula—

namely : [image] etc.

It is evident that this is merely a *difference to the eye,* but not to the ear, as the low B flat of the Great Organ *does "speak"* by means of the pedal coupling. The advantage of the form suggested lies in the non-interference of the left hand with the key pulled down by the pedal. When such a unison-meeting of finger and pedal occurs upon a given key, the sensation, as most organists are aware, is not a pleasant one.

Sustaining or repeating the same Pedal tone.

As a general rule, when the same pedal tone fills two or more successive measures, it may be continuously sustained from measure to measure, provided the rhythm is sufficiently marked in the other parts. This can not be the case here, as it is the bass to which we look for the rhythmic accent principally.   For this reason, the pedal tone is to be repeated in each measure, and if the rhythmic effect still be deemed insufficient, the following pedal form may be resorted

to—namely : 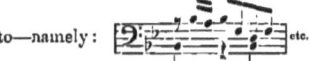 etc.

These forms of simplifying a florid orchestral bass for the organ are generally preferable to performing the passage as written; although an expert organist, possessed of sufficient pedal execution, may, in rare instances, be justified in playing them literally.

EXAMPLE 99.

HAYDN. 3D MASS.

Quo - - ni - am   tu   so - lus sanc - tus, etc.

The above example comes under the same head as the previous one. In place of the ascending scale with which the orchestral basses begin the movement, the pedals of the organ give the vocal bass in the lower octave. In this example, it will be noticed that there is no interference between the left hand and such keys as may be affected by the Great to Pedal coupler.

It occasionally happens that formulas of accompaniment which (transcribed from the original orchestral score) are given in their piano-forte setting to the right hand, may, in case of the organ, be given to the left hand in preference. *Transposition of Motion from Right to Left hand.*

Thus, in the following example, the common figure at *a* (Example 100) may change its form, when executed, to that at *b*.

EXAMPLE 100.

It is especially useful to adopt the organ form at *b* as a substitute for the piano form given at *a*, whenever a closely connected legato is desired, while yet the sense of motion is to remain unimpaired. This is easily accomplished if two manuals be employed, that for the left hand being registered slightly louder, while the sustained tones may even have a four-foot stop of mild intonation added to them. The justification of the change of figure at *b* from the form at *a* will, perhaps, be understood better if we give the orchestral form from which Example 100, *a*, has been derived—the scoring being extremely simple. *Example of Orchestral Derivation.*

EXAMPLE 101.

The form of arpeggio chosen as a piano adaptation, in Example 100, *a*, gives the fifth as its highest note. This, so far as may be, through use of the pedal, corresponds with the sustained tones of the wind instruments shown in Example 101, while yet its principal mission is to give the rhythmic motion.

At *b*, Example 100, the organ form is seen to approach more nearly to the orchestral effect. The two sustained tones ⟦♪⟧ give, with the addition of a four-foot stop, their octaves, thus: ⟦♪⟧ This corresponds exactly (in pitch, but not in quality, of course) with the tones sustained by the Flutes, Clarionets, 1st Horn and 1st Bassoon, in Example 101. The tones represented by the 2d Horn and 2d Bassoon can not be sustained, but are virtually given in the arpeggio upon the other manual, in connection with the pedal. The form of the arpeggio (Example 100, *b*) is seen to be taken from the 1st Violin part (Example 101), played in the lower octave. By the use of two manuals, as here designed, it would be possible in this instance to play all the string parts literally, as well as give the sustained wind tones. This may not unfrequently be feasible, but the additional difficulty of performance does not, as a rule, render such treatment desirable. Such a form as that at *b*, Example 100, suffices.

Without entering into the complex subject of orchestral scoring, it is seen, by Example 101, that in the orchestra the figuration falls ordinarily to the lot of the stringed instruments, but the sustained notes to the wind, according to their nature, the result being the unity of repose and motion.

Procedure in case of a Piano-forte Adaptation. In making a piano-forte adaptation, the figuration is the first thing transcribed, together with the bass. Then follow such hints of the sustained (filling-in) harmonies as the nature of the piece and the nature of the piano will allow. It is clear that with the organ, especially through the use of the obligato pedal, we can accomplish more. Of the piano form of adaptation, Example 100, *a*, furnishes the simplest possible illustration, but the student must remember that the accompaniments to all the oratorios, masses, etc., are, as a rule, nothing but similarly derived *piano* accompaniments. It remains, then, for him, when again re-adapting them for the organ, to supply the lack of sustained tones, which tones really exist in the original orchestral form, either above, below, or buried in the midst of the harmony.

As the majority of organists make no study of orchestral scores, it becomes a matter of judgment as to *what* tones shall be sustained. The author hopes that this chapter may furnish some hints to this end, for the use of those who have no time, nor, perhaps, inclination to acquire the requisite knowledge through means of a sufficient study of instrumentation itself.

EXAMPLE 102.

"CREDO," BEETHOVEN. MASS IN C.

At *a*, in the above example, the piano form establishes the motion, both by the regularly pulsating F♯ in the bass, and also by the tremolo which here lies between melody and bass.

At *b*, the organ form of the same example, we retain two sustained tones, which, with the melody, produces an independent three-part harmony. The repetition of the F♯, here absolutely necessary to the establishment of the marked rhythm desired, is carried out in a much more effective way than the piano form of the same thing—namely, by the pedal in the lower octave played staccato. The tremolo or prolonged shake, coming between the legato melody and the two sustained tones, may be retained literally with good effect. Thus, the organ form comes much nearer the orchestral original, even when we leave out all considerations of registration, as the required motion is preserved upon the one hand, while, upon the other, the sustained tones give the passage an inner unity which the piano form fails to accomplish even with the use of the pedal.

Motion in the middle parts with more than one sustained tone.

EXAMPLE 103.

BEETHOVEN. MASS IN C.

The literal performance upon the organ of piano accompaniments similar to the above always sounds badly, even if one or two sustained tones are substituted for the continual repetitions in the left hand. The effect of the diminished chord, taken by the left hand so low down

Inversion of the accompanimental Chord.

upon the organ, is not only gloomy in itself, but it is here diametrically opposed to the original orchestral setting, which is transparent and clear in effect. This is not owing simply to the *quality of tone* produced by stringed instruments (to which this tremolo is given) as opposed to wind instruments, but rather to the different inversion of the accompanying chord. In such cases as the previous one, this inversion would usually be given in the orchestra as follows :

The impossibility of executing this upon the piano with the left hand, while the right is occupied with the figuration proper, is the excuse for giving it in the particular form as seen at Example 103.

The organist is better off in this respect, for, having the pedals at his disposal, and the scope of his left hand thus largely increased, he can *restore* the chord, if not to its original inversion, at least to an inversion approaching the proper effect. To be able to detect the origin of such piano-forte forms, and give a *good* organ equivalent for them, is an accomplishment which every organist who is called upon to play accompaniments of this class should possess.

Possibilities upon the Organ.

Neither is it absolutely necessary to have a knowledge of what the orchestral scoring of the passage may be. It suffices to have a realizing sense of that dispersion of the harmony which is best suited to the nature of the composition—as we say a piece is "well put upon the instrument." In this instance, the organ form of Example 103 may be given thus :

EXAMPLE 104.

Here we have three sustained tones, two in the manual and one in the pedal, the rhythm being well established by the figuration itself.* If the preceding example were to be played upon *two* manuals, the left hand might well assume the inversion  etc.

Other forms might be employed as follows, according to the sense of greater or lesser motion required :

EXAMPLE 105.

Varieties of Inversion, and their Conditions.

The choice of the particular form in this and similar cases will be governed largely by the amount of motion which the right hand may have allotted to it. It is evident that the more sustained tones we have, the more the motion becomes subordinated. Likewise, if the motion is to assert itself rather distinctly, it can best do so when the sustained tones are *beneath it* rather than over it. This can readily be demonstrated at the organ.

* In this connection, see remarks on " sustaining or repeating the same pedal tone," under Example 98.

Referring again to Example 103, it will be seen that the accompaniment changes from *piano* to *forte* to meet the alternation of solo and chorus. If the Swell Organ be used for the whole passage, it will be too weak for the chorus. If the Great Organ is used throughout, it will be too powerful for the solo accompaniment. This necessitates a change of manuals in the midst of the passage, which must still retain its legato character. It may be accomplished thus :

EXAMPLE 106.

The opening is seen to be upon the Swell "both hands." The last three notes of the right hand, in the first measure, *anticipate the forte* of the following measure, besides forming an effective leading to the D♭ of the second measure upon which the Sopranos enter. *With the accent of the second measure*, the left hand is also transferred to the Great Organ, reinforcing the chorus entrance. At the beginning of the third measure, the order of transfer is reversed, the left hand returning to the Swell *with* the measure, while the right lingers upon the Great Organ the duration of one sixteenth note ♫. In this particular instance, this one loud tone is rather welcome than otherwise, as it both covers and assists the Solo Soprano's entrance, which is here somewhat difficult as respects intonation.

One other problem here presents itself—namely, as to how the Pedal is to be registered. If coupled with the Great Organ, it will be too powerful for the solo ; if only with the Swell, or not coupled at all, the instrumental bass will not properly support the chorus.

If the organ is provided with a reversible pedal to bring on and throw off the Great to Pedal Coupler, as happily most of our modern instruments are (and *always should be*), the matter becomes simple enough. As it is evident, from the nature of the passage, that the left hand can not be spared to draw the coupler in default of the above arrangement (and our older organs do not possess it), it is preferable to dispense with it at the chorus points rather than mutilate the solo passages. In other words, not to couple with the Great Organ at all. An intelligent pupil should be able, after a careful examination of the previous example, to apply the principle therein contained to hundreds of analogous cases. It is hardly necessary to say that, in many instances, only the *simultaneous* shifting of hands from one manual to another will properly express the contrast of *forte* and *piano* required.

EXAMPLE 107.

BEETHOVEN. MASS IN C.

Example 107, given in its piano form, affords another illustration of the advisability of inverting the left-hand chords when played upon the organ.* Either of the two following inversions may be employed:  The passage is, by its nature, best suited to solo treatment, and therefore to the use of two manuals—the right hand upon the Swell and the left upon the Choir or Great Organ until the double asterisk (**). From this point, both hands should unite upon the Swell.

Legato Octave Passages in Skips.

Octave passages of the character of the melody in Example 107 may usually be rendered legato (when executed *forte* upon the Great Organ) by a substitution of the left hand for the right in playing some of the lower tones of the octave passage. This is shown at *a* in the following example:

EXAMPLE 108.

Octaves by means of Four-foot Registration.

The problem offered in Example 107 is, however, that of a solo passage in octaves, with the accompaniment upon a second manual. The octaves, as they there occur, are practically impossible to render in a true legato manner upon the organ, on account of the awkward skips occurring in the melody. As the passage is to be held *piano* throughout, it is advisable to execute it by playing the lower notes of the octave passage upon the Swell, *but with four-foot stops drawn*, in addition to the eight-foot stops, thus giving the octave desired. In cases similar to the above, the resumption of both hands upon one manual, as at the double asterisk (Example 108, *b*), had better be made upon the Choir or Great Organ, if the four-foot tone is there to be avoided.

The multitude of forms of piano accompaniment which may be adapted to the organ, more or less successfully, render it impracticable to add more than a few additional illustrations on this subject. The majority of examples which may present themselves to the student will, as a rule, be found to range themselves under some one of the general heads already considered. The rest must be left to the student's own invention and talent, guided by the general principles we have attempted to deduce.

We close this chapter with several illustrations from Rossini's "Stabat Mater:"

---

* It is not to be understood that *all* chords written low down in the manual compass are to be inverted. The player must be governed by the character of the composition, and of course by the orchestral original, if he can ascertain what that is.

EXAMPLE 109.

Comparison of the two forms *a* and *b* shows various differences.

1. The omission of the melody as given in the piano form. Here, it will be remembered that it is only a quartet of solo voices which is accompanied.*

2. The repetition of [notation] as given in the piano form is omitted at *b*. On the other hand, the *third of the chord* (B♭), which is lacking in the first measure at *a*, is here restored.

3. The essential rhythm is decided by the pedal beat at *b*.

Comparison of Piano and Organ Forms.

EXAMPLE 110.

* See remarks on repetition of melody in the accompaniment of solo voices. Chapter VII., page 68.

At *a*, Example 110, we have the form of piano accompaniment as transcribed from the orchestral score.

Inversion with sustained Tones and Syncopation. At *b*, we note the inversion of the chord as better suited to the organ, and more nearly approaching the orchestral original. The effect of the holding tone (F) should also be noticed, by means of which the broken effect is mitigated for the organ. In spite of this tone, the *continued* syncopation of the right against the left hand becomes almost too unorganlike, and the following may be suggested as preferable, while doing no violence to the composer's intention :

The following example from the well-known "Inflammatus" is of peculiar difficulty, and yet frequently falls to the lot of organists to accompany :

EXAMPLE 111.

The figuration of the accompaniment is here peculiarly effective for stringed instruments, and for nothing else. Upon the piano the continual recurrence of the above form is fatiguing. Upon the organ no less so, with the additional drawback that the rapid repetitions of the same chord are still more foreign to the nature of the instrument. Notwithstanding this, the original figuration characterizes the accompaniment to such a degree that it is here out of the question to omit it, at least in the beginning. Subsequently, the following simplification may be adopted

after the entrance of the voice—namely : 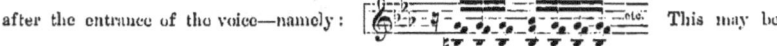 This may be

the more readily employed where the *chorus* voices enter *piano*. (See the piano score of the "Stabat Mater," at the words, "*fac me cruce custodiri*," etc.)

The small notes (Example 111) represent the chords softly sustained upon a second manual. This treatment should be continued throughout, wherever the figuration of Example 111 occurs, except in the *f* and *ff* passages where the Great Organ is employed. In this latter case, the sustained tones will follow the analogy of Example 90 or 91, or the sustained tones may be given to the left hand.

At the climax of the *solo*, the Great Organ (both hands) may be required. Previous to this, the following form may be adopted as an organ equivalent. It has the advantage of allowing the accompanist to follow with ease the slight *accelerando* which the singer, almost instinctively,

falls into at this point of the solo. It is also easier for the right hand to join the left upon
the Great Organ at the climax of the solo " *in die judicii.*" (See piano score of "Stabat
Mater.") The change to the Great Organ from the form employed at Example 111 would
evidently be abrupt, the right hand there resting upon the Swell and the left upon the Choir
Organ.

EXAMPLE 112.

On accompanying the duet, "*Quis est homo?*" from the same "Stabat," the essential Cases where
Inversion is to
be avoided.
figure [musical figure] is accompanied in the piano score by harmonies generally lying
at about this range—namely: [musical figure]   This would seem to warrant the inversion of the
chord held upon the second manual on the principle advanced in the remarks under Example 103,
although, in the case referred to, the chord was a "diminished" one. This will be found less
advisable in case of the duet mentioned, on account of certain chromatic progressions of the two
voices which the student will do well to examine in the work itself. Should the chord of the
second manual be placed in a higher inversion, as, for instance. [musical figure] it might be
found to interfere with and blur the clear progression of the two voices.

In all these cases of accompanimental adaptation, a proper conception of qualifying condi- "Drum-rolls."
tions is indispensable—not the mechanical adoption of a formula, which, considered by itself,
may be well enough, but from the vocal stand-point quite objectionable.

In orchestral adaptations, we not unfrequently meet with passages which, in the original,
were merely a roll upon the kettle-drums. This is represented upon the piano by an octave
tremolo in the bass. This effect is, of course, wholly foreign to the organ. An illustration of
this is the opening of the Bass solo, "*Pro peccatis.*" About the best approach to the effect
desired may be accomplished thus :

EXAMPLE 113.

This illustration will be seen to differ
from Example 94, at *c*, in that the pedal
does not possess the octave lower than the
manual. For this reason, the Pedal and
Great Organ *are not coupled*. The sixteen-
foot tone only is heard from the pedal,
while the rapidly recurring dissonance of
the G# with it produces, as near as may
be, some resemblance to the "drum-roll."

If a manual-stop of sixteen feet be also employed, the effect will be all the better. The *sustained* pedal note prevents the clashing of the dissonance with it from disturbing unduly our sense of tonic foundation.

In concluding this chapter, even the tyro in the art of accompaniment must feel that we have scarcely passed the threshold of the subject, important as it is. We may as well pause here, however, as the art of successful adaptation is so largely a matter of talent and musical instinct, governed, indeed, by certain general principles which we have striven to elucidate in the previous pages.

CHAPTER X.

THE great value of the Swell Organ to the accompanist is evidently its capability of producing expressive effects. Such effects are only attainable upon the Great or Choir Organs through the addition or withdrawal of stops, and this method (as we have before seen, Chapter III.) is attended with two drawbacks: (1) the necessity of removing one hand from the manual to accomplish the change of stops, and (2) a certain abruptness of effect which can not be entirely overcome, even by the most skilful registration. *The Swell as a means of Expression.*

On the other hand, the Swell Organ possesses the advantage of equality and gradation of tone within the limits of crescendo and diminuendo possible to it. This renders it peculiarly valuable in solo accompaniments, and others where a frequently varying power is required, but not exceeding mezzo-forte.

Considered as a separate organ, the Swell will naturally be treated upon the same principle as the other manuals, so far as combination and building up of tone are concerned. It remains, then, to notice certain peculiarities attending its use, resulting mainly from its local position within the organ, and from the nature of its construction.

For the benefit of those who may be ignorant *how* the Swell effect is produced, we devote a few words of explanation by way of preliminary. The pipes of the Swell Organ are inclosed within a box which is furnished with movable blinds or shutters, the same being sometimes made double. These blinds are placed at the front of the Swell-box, facing out into the church, and thus forming the only point of exit for the tone, except so far as it penetrates the box itself, wood being an excellent sound-conductor. To overcome this tendency last referred to, and confine the sound within the box (except as it may be emitted at the desired opening), the box itself is frequently lined within with pasteboard or some other partially non-conducting material. The Swell Pedal opens and closes the blinds. When the pedal is pressed down, opening the blinds, it is evident that we shall have the *fortissimo* of the Swell, while, when the pedal is up (blinds closed), we shall have the Swell *pianissimo*. All the varied gradations between these two points will depend (1) upon the number and voicing of the Swell-stops, (2) upon the tightness with which the blinds shut in the tone, and, lastly (3), upon the situation of the Swell itself as related to the general acoustic properties of the church. *How the Swell effect is produced.*

The box containing the Swell Organ is usually placed above the Great and Choir Organs. This elevation, and the fact of the inclosure of the pipes, leads to a few remarks which we would commend to the attention of inexperienced players. *Effect of Elevation upon the Swell.*

The elevation of the Swell subjects it to a higher temperature than the rest of the organ, especially in winter-time under furnace heat, or in case of an evening service when a large audience is present, and much gas burned. The metal pipes are the most sensitive to this (notably the reeds), the effect being that of an expansion of the metal, which, in turn, is *equivalent to a lengthening of the pipe*. Thus, the pipes which are subjected to such influence will soon be found "flat," as compared with the rest of the organ. This will be particularly noticed when the Great and Swell, or the Swell and Choir, are coupled together. The only resource of the organist in such cases is to use these respective manuals separately without coupling. When a church has been rather cold, and the heat rises very rapidly under the combined influence of a large congregation and many gas-burners, he may even be obliged to forego all use of the Swell. In ordinary cases, where the discrepancy is noticed, the use of the different manuals without coupling may be adopted with comparative impunity; as a change of manuals from Great *to* Swell, or *vice versa*, will be far less noticeable as regards tune than the effect of Great *and* Swell coupled together. In this latter case, the ear is compelled to notice and compare the unisons of the two manuals, while in the former case the pipes of the two organs may remain in tolerable tune *with those of their own manual*, but disagree with another manual.

Conditions of Temperature affecting "Coupling."

When the Organ stands in a Recess.

When the organ stands in a recess, in the rear of which the Swell has its position, the reverse of the above will not unfrequently be noticed. The heat rising from the body of the church first affects the metal pipes of the Great Organ which are exposed in front. The Swell, meantime, standing well back in the recess, is filled with colder air, and is sometimes very slow in attaining the same temperature as the front of the organ. This will be the case, especially if the Swell-blinds are left closed when the heat first begins to rise. For this reason, the Swell Pedal *should always be fastened down on leaving the instrument*, in order that the temperature of the Swell may rise and fall as equally as possible with that of the other portions of the organ.

It is among organs which stand in a recess that we most frequently hear glaring discrepancies between Swell and Great Organ. The Swell is apt not to become affected by the outside rising temperature until that temperature is decidedly high—that is, relatively so. The Swell then begins to change rapidly, which has the additional fault of throwing its pipes out of tune with each other, not to speak of its disagreement with the Great and Choir Organs.

Mode of Equalizing the Temperature.

One means of partially avoiding this annoyance is to open the doors of the Swell-box in the rear as well as the shutters in front for an hour previous to using the instrument, while the heat is rising. A lower door or panel of the organ-case may also be opened to aid in equalizing the circulation of air. In some large organs, where gas has been introduced into the Swell-box (for convenience in tuning, in place of using portable lights or candles), the burners may sometimes be used for heating purposes, as they will soon change the temperature within the Swell, especially if it is rising outside.

Effect of Elevation upon the "carrying over" of Tone.

The other effect of the elevation of the Swell which concerns the player is the "carrying over" of the tone which frequently occurs. This characteristic renders it important that the organist should know the effect of the soft stops of the Swell as heard at a distance from the keys. He should be able to realize their effect individually, and that of their combination with each other and with voices. Neglect of this point is the most fruitful cause of "over-accompanying," especially in case of solo voices. This quality of carrying-over tone may generally be esteemed a good trait, as such organs prove most effective to the majority of listeners rather than to those in immediate proximity to the instrument. It is evident that it requires the organist to be especially careful of the proportions of tone to be employed.

Instances also occur where the effect will be almost directly opposite to that just spoken of. By some latent defect in the acoustic of the church, or miscalculation on the part of the organ-builder, the instrument may seem powerful and brilliant at the keys, but unaccountably muffled in tone and generally ineffective in the body of the church. In such cases, a somewhat stronger registration may be required to balance the voices properly.

The most lamentable result which can occur in Swell accompaniment is the following—namely: when the location of the Swell and the acoustic qualities of the church combine to " carry over " the tone to such a degree that a solo voice (or quartet of voices) scarcely perceives the tone of the organ when played softly, thus rendering the intonation uncertain.

In such a case, the organist is placed in the following awkward dilemma: (1.) If he accompanies softly, he may not meet the requirements of the voices as to support. (2.) On the other hand, if he accompanies so that the singers feel no more than comfortably supported, the effect in the church will be that of " over-accompaniment " previously referred to. The only hope of attaining a proper musical effect when thus hampered, is to have voices capable of singing all the softer passages with correct intonation and virtually without accompaniment. If the singers are found competent to do this, the organist has but to ascertain the proper amount of accompaniment to give a "*piano*" or "*mezzo-piano*" effect, as heard by the congregation; even if to himself and the choir the accompaniment seem quite inadequate. Fortunately, extreme cases of this kind are not frequent, but they are by no means so rare as not to deserve consideration.

The expressive use of the Swell is liable to one very common abuse, which may best be expressed by the common term "*sawing* upon the Swell Pedal." When inexperienced players find their right foot upon this pedal, something seems to prompt them to keep it constantly in motion. The result is, of course, a monotonous ⟨ ⟩ generally aggravated by a series of little jerks, wholly unrelated to the natural expression which the phrase may require. In case of our older organs, this habit was the more easily fallen into by beginners, on account of the comparatively primitive construction of the Swell Pedal and its mechanism. This required the performer to keep his right foot continuously upon the pedal, with the exception of such passages as might be executed with the Swell entirely closed or wholly open. A " *mezzo-forte* " with most of the Swell-stops drawn (for instance), could only be obtained by keeping the pedal in position by the continued use of the right foot.

Of late years, our best organ-builders have introduced vastly improved styles of Swell Pedal, even in case of their smaller instruments. These are (1) the *balanced* Swell Pedal, and (2) the " *Ratchet* " Pedal. Both of these give the organist the power of making a partial crescendo or diminuendo (within the limits of the Swell's capacity), and leaving the pedal *fixed* at whatever point the foot may be removed from it.

As to the means by which this is effected, we have not space to particularize here the mechanism of the two species of pedals referred to. Suffice it to say that the " Balanced " Pedal derives its name from weights or balances, affecting the Swell-blinds in such a way that their opening or closing may be controlled and suspended at any desired point. The " Ratchet " Pedal accomplishes the same result in a different way. Here there is a little pedal or lever within, or placed upon the top of the Swell Pedal proper, both of which are simultaneously operated by the foot. After pressing the pedal down (opening the blinds) to a suitable degree of power, the heel is dropped an inch or two. This allows the small lever to rise independently, and its motion inserts a wooden or metal tongue into the " ratchet " (or series of notches) just within the organ-case, thus holding the pedal at the point arrived at. To have the pedal pass rapidly from pp to $f\!f$, one

Other Effects of Locality.

Improper use of the Swell Pedal.

The " Balanced " Swell.

The " Ratchet " Pedal.

has only to avoid dropping the heel.   Care must be exercised, in pressing the pedal down, not to allow the tongue referred to to strike against the notches, producing an unpleasantly audible clicking sound, which is due only to the awkwardness of the performer.   This can not occur if the heel is not dropped while pressing the pedal down.

Technique of the "Balanced" Swell Pedal.

The above unpleasant possibility can not occur in case of the "Balanced" Swell Pedal.   On the other hand, the latter being equipoised, sometimes moves so easily that the foot, feeling next to no resistance, will allow the Swell-blinds to open or close too rapidly, passing beyond the point desired in either direction.   Any tendency of this kind may usually be conquered by a slightly increased pressure of the foot upon the pedal.   This may the more readily be accomplished as the "Balanced" Pedal admits of the whole foot being placed firmly upon it, after the manner of the blowing treadle in reed organs.   The motion should be controlled solely by the flexibility of the ankle, without undue knee motion.

Varied situation of the Swell Pedal.

The "Ratchet" Pedal is placed at the extreme right of the pedal keyboard, as in case of the old-fashioned, uncontrollable Swell.

The "Balanced" Pedal, on the contrary, is not unfrequently met with in our most recent organs, placed in the centre, over the pedal keyboard.   This has two advantages: Firstly, in being nearer, and therefore more convenient to the performer's right foot; not necessitating the outstretching of the right leg, which frequently becomes tiresome in the old style of pedals, especially when they chance to be somewhat heavily weighted.   Secondly, when placed in the centre, it never interferes with the execution of passages upon the pedal keyboard.   This trouble not unfrequently occurs upon the extreme high pedal keys when the Swell Pedal is of the old or even ratchet pattern, and is "fastened down."

Drawback to central position of "Balanced" Pedal.

One drawback to these advantages possessed by the "Balanced" Pedal is the following : When a passage requires the right foot to remain upon the Swell Pedal for the sake of varying expression, and the bass is given to the left foot to execute in the *second* octave of the pedal keyboard, a more or less awkward relation of the two feet must ensue.   This may be overcome by a little practice on the part of such organists as may possess a Balanced Pedal located in the centre, by substituting the *left* foot to control the Swell during such passages, and executing the bass with the right.

A consideration of this last case (which may well occur in modern organ-playing and be employed in accompaniment) shows that this improved pedal now brings with it *a new technique*, if we may so call it.   An illustration follows, the Balanced Pedal being supposed to *occupy the centre* over the pedal keyboard.

EXAMPLE 114.

Mode of applying the above "new technique."

Here, it would be manifestly impossible to manage the Swell Pedal properly with the right foot, if in the centre, owing to the impracticable relations it would be forced to sustain with the

* The signs o and v denote respectively the heel and toe.

left. If the Swell Pedal is situated on the extreme right, the left foot might execute the bass passage.

Another advantage arising from the improved form of Swell Pedal is the possibility which now exists in the legato execution of bass passages in which skips occur. As the pedal will remain in any desired position, the right foot can be momentarily spared to assist the left in the legato rendering of a phrase, until the right foot is obliged to return to the Swell Pedal to modify the power of the Swell. This may occur upon a single note only. *Improved facilities in legato pedal-playing by means of these pedals.*

EXAMPLE 115.

A glance at the above example will show the impossibility of executing it properly upon an organ furnished with the old-fashioned Swell Pedal, and yet composers constantly call for such effects. Without a " Balanced " or " Ratchet " Pedal, it would become necessary at the points *a*, *b*, *c*, *d*, to break the legato phrase in the bass, and allow the *left* foot to spring to the following key. If this were *not* done, but two feet employed, the Swell would either have to be fully opened or completely closed (and this latter after having once begun the crescendo !), in order to free the right foot. *Disadvantages of the old method.*

As it is (Example 115), the crescendo begins very gradually during the first measure. With the first note of the second measure, the right foot assumes the bass, the Swell meantime remaining at the power thus far attained. At the second note of the second measure, both feet have *simultaneous* duties—namely : the left foot resumes the bass part, and, at the same moment, the right returns to the Swell Pedal. With the accent of the following (third) measure, the crescendo is renewed, leading to the climax with fully opened blinds at the fourth measure. The following diminuendo, being accomplished by the same mechanical treatment, needs no special comment. *Crescendo and Diminuendo by means of the " Balanced " or " Ratchet " Pedal.*

It will have been noticed that at measures 2 and 4, no crescendo was made, the right foot having, in both instances, been momentarily employed with the bass part. This does not materially affect the impression which the ear receives of gradual increase of power, as the opening of the Swell-blinds is instantly resumed in the following measure, and there is, at least, no falling off in quantity of tone—as there would be, if freeing the right foot involved closing the Swell again, while the right foot was otherwise employed. *When " Breaks " are permissible in Crescendo or Diminuendo.*

The gradual crescendo may be produced with even greater smoothness when the duration of the bass notes permits a rapid substitution of one foot for the other. For instance, had the bass part at measure 2 been written thus, [notation] the right foot would then strike the E flat, but the left be instantly substituted for it, without allowing the note to repeat itself, thus freeing the right again to return instantly to the Swell Pedal.

A careful examination of the two preceding examples, and the principles they involve, should sufficiently illustrate what we have termed the "new" technique of the improved Swell Pedal. This mechanical improvement requires far more study in gaining expert command of both feet, and the Swell effects thus made possible, than is usually given to it. Study in this direction, however, will be amply rewarded by an artistic result, from which the organist was, until of late years, wholly precluded by the shortcomings of the instrument itself.

The improved Swell Pedal as a means of Registration. Besides the improved application of effects in crescendo and diminuendo which the modern Swell Pedal gives us, it also opens up entirely new possibilities in the way of Swell registration, particularly as applied to the accompaniment of solo-stops or solo-voices, the latter more especially when two manuals are to be employed. Let us endeavor to make clear in what manner these new sources of registration may be obtained through means of a Balanced Swell. We may, perhaps, accomplish this the more easily if we first consider the drawbacks attending the use of the old style of Swell Pedal.

Dilemmas in Registration with the old-fashioned Swell Pedal. Suppose we desire to contrast two qualities of tone (say Flute and Reed tone) upon two manuals, it being understood that the two voices are to measurably balance each other as to power. We draw an eight-foot Flute (Melodia) upon the Choir or Great Organ, and upon the Swell the Oboe, with possibly the Stopped Diapason added to give body to the reed. To the left hand we assign the Swell, with the reed in Tenor range, as being there most characteristic in quality. For a similar reason, we assign the Choir or Great Organ to the right hand and a higher range of compass.

Now, if to the above conditions we add that of an obligato pedal part, demanding the use of both feet, although of ever so simple a character as to passage-playing, how could we properly execute this upon an organ provided only with the old-fashioned pedal?

In the first place, if the Swell-box remained closed, we should find that the Oboe did not balance the bright-toned Flute with its higher range. To remedy this, it would be necessary to open the Swell somewhat. To keep the Swell a little open, however, we should be obliged to devote the right foot to that purpose. What, then, becomes of the obligato pedal part, if, as the chances are, it can not be executed properly by the left foot alone?

On the other hand, if the Swell Pedal be fastened down, giving the full force of the Swell stops mentioned, the reed may be found to overbalance the Flute.

Quantity at the Expense of Quality. What was the old method of procedure? Perhaps to add the Dulciana and Flute, four feet, to the Choir or Great Organ. Then, very likely, the Swell, in turn overbalanced, had the Open Diapason added to it with or without its own Dulciana, and thus the *balance* required was measurably attained. A moment's thought, or, better yet, practical experiment, will show that this result was obtained at the expense of *contrasting quality*. The result at which we have arrived is that of a *combination* of one manual against that of another, which, however they may balance as to power, produce conjointly a very different effect from that proposed in the original problem. This, as it will be remembered, was the contrasting of two radically distinct *qualities* of tone. This will never show itself so plainly as when we have a representative stop upon each manual, differing in character, but blending together in harmonic union.

The worst feature, then, of the old Swell Pedal, was the necessity it laid upon us of smothering characteristic quality by adding a number of stops with the Swell closed, if it were desired to balance a relatively bright but not powerful Flute combination upon another manual.

This was nearly always the case when the pedal part called for the use of both feet, and led to a mutilation of such pedal parts by an attempt to play the bass with one foot.

. With the improved Swell Pedal, nothing is easier than to permanently set the Swell blinds —a third, half, or two thirds open, thus freeing both feet for necessary use. This is an effect wholly distinct from the primary use of the pedal. It is, indeed, equivalent to the power of changing temporarily the voicing of certain stops, so that they may be for the moment better fitted to accomplish certain specific duties.

Advantage of being able to " set " the Swell.

We have spoken of the gain derived from being able to use the softer stops with the Swell blinds set partially open. It is self-evident that another class of results may be produced by approximately *closing* the Swell with the louder stops drawn, as the Open Diapason, Principal, Cornopean (or Trumpet), etc.

The following example, taken from Hesse's " Theme and Variations," Op. 47, is given as a practical illustration of the advantages of the Balanced Swell. The pupil may experiment with various combinations of stops and " settings " of the Swell Pedal, as well as use the latter expressively. The melody is in the left hand and should predominate somewhat.

EXAMPLE 116.

Illustrations in the mode of setting the Swell Pedal referred to as applied to accompaniment may be found in many previous examples. See more especially Chapter VIII. on obligato accompaniment.

When the Swell is *continously* used as a means of expression, the organist is forced to keep his right foot upon the pedal, and in this respect the Balanced Swell offers no particular advantage over the old style—unless it be placed over the centre of the pedal keyboard.

Use of the Left Foot. When necessitated.

A certain special expertness with the left foot is therefore demanded, in order that the bass may be as smoothly executed as possible. The mere touching key after key with the toe of the left foot does not cover the case at all. The alternate use of toe and heel must here be made the most of, so that as few breaks as possible may occur. Although it is foreign to the purpose of this work to introduce technical studies for the organ, yet we venture to add, the following exercises for the benefit of such students as may require them, and who desire to acquire the legato use of the left foot speedily.

EXAMPLE 117.

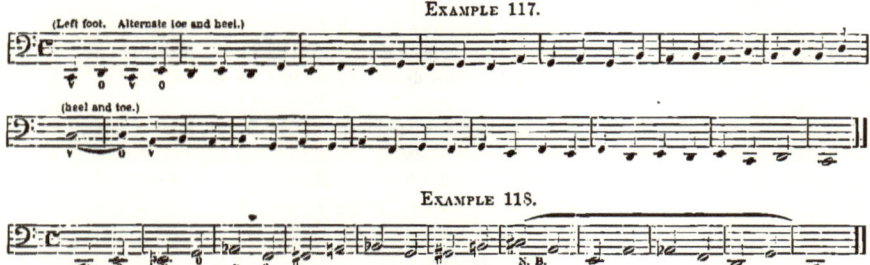

EXAMPLE 118.

Thirds and Fourths with the Left Foot.   Both of these exercises are to be practised in the strictest *legato*. Example 118 is specially calculated to give elasticity to the ankle. There should be as little motion of the knee as possible, the foot being turned to the right and left as though upon a pivot, which is represented by the heel. At N.B., this is specially illustrated. When the heel descends upon the second note of that measure (A), the toe should instantly swing round to be ready for the coming E of the following measure.

EXAMPLE 119.

At * a perfect legato can not be preserved. Here the advantage of a balanced pedal is evident. With this at command, the Swell can be left without reduction or addition of power. The right foot substitutes momentarily for the left upon the C, enabling the left foot to descend to F. Upon this, the right foot resumes the pedal for the decrescendo.

The Swell as a means of securing Intonation.   The student of accompaniments should not overlook another and very important use of the Swell—namely: its power of restoring or sustaining a wavering intonation on the part of singers. In this respect, it is invaluable, as a slight increase of power, promptly applied, will frequently be sufficient to steady a voice in this particular.

The addition of a four-foot stop on any manual will usually help a singer who begins to " flat ;" the octave tone materially assisting the sense of pitch. If suddenly introduced, however, it may prove obtrusive. Upon the Swell, we have the double advantage of being able to control the power of the added stop by means of the pedal, and, secondly, the voicing and local position of the Swell is such (as we have previously seen) that the addition of the four-foot stops does not have the radical effect of the Great or Choir Organs. Besides this, we can "meet" the addition of the Swell four-foot stops by a slight decrescendo upon the Swell Pedal, by which the power is not increased, but the higher registration simply gives a keener sense of the tonality.

It is to be understood that we do not refer to the use of a four-foot stop in a combination *appropriate to it*, but rather to its addition to a combination, which, properly speaking, might be better off without it. The addition referred to is that of a four-foot stop or stops to an already satisfactory eight-foot combination, and for the sole purpose of securing the intonation.

This will often be found effectual if the singer does not frequently or habitually sing " out of tune." When a vocalist has the habit of singing "sharp" rather than "flat," it is far more difficult, if not impossible, for the accompanist to assist him or her. The crescendo of the Swell and addition of a four-foot stop will sometimes accomplish the desired effect, but will too often prove fruitless.

Singers who "sharp" rather than "flat."

The reason of this is apparently the following: A singer of some musical sensibility, feeling the crescendo of the Swell and general increase of power, instinctively sings with a little more force. This has a tendency, if any thing, to raise the pitch, and thus the singer who may be "flat" has a chance of recovering his or her intonation. For the same reason, the singer who is already above the correct intonation is not apt to fall in pitch upon hearing the increased power, but rather to remain confirmed in his or her fault.

One thing may safely be asserted—namely: that if the increased power and higher registration combined do not restore a singer's intonation, within a measure or two, the organist should resort to precisely the opposite treatment. It is of no use to call the listener's attention to a discrepancy between voice and instrument. Besides which, curiously enough, it sometimes happens that the singer, missing the full support which preceded the organist's sudden diminuendo, *listens*, and—regains the true pitch.

Opposite Treatment.

The above treatment of the Swell, as relates to intonation, is more particularly applicable to solo accompaniment, or to assist the Soprano in a quartet. Should a Tenor voice, singing in quartet, require special support, it is best effected by playing the part upon another manual. This is the only manner in which a middle part could be made to predominate so as to be felt by the singer.

In some small organs, not particularly well appointed, it will sometimes be noticed in effects requiring the use of the Full Swell that it gives too great a sense of the upper octaves—the four-foot stops, Mixture, etc., asserting themselves too radically.

Of the Full Swell in small Organs.

In such a case, if the organ possess a good Melodia (or Doppel-Flöte) on the Great Organ, the Swell may advantageously be coupled to it. It will give the Swell "body," and yet be wholly absorbed by it as to quality. Neither will it affect its capability of effect in crescendo and diminuendo.

Were the Great Open Diapason chosen instead of the Melodia, it would assert its own powerful quality, which, though good in itself, would not become absorbed as a constituent part of the swell tone proper.

CHAPTER XI.

INTERLUDES.

Objections to
their use.
INTERLUDES are, as a rule, an abomination. From an æsthetic stand-point, they rarely form a connecting link between the verses of a hymn, while from a technical (musical) point of view, they are usually trash.

It is a difficult thing to say any thing *extempore* (that is worth hearing) in the exceedingly short time that the interlude should occupy. If, on the other hand, the interlude be musically good, but of excessive length, the result is nearly as lamentable. On the result when, at one and the same time, the length is great, and the matter presented is poor, we need not dwell.

It is a matter of congratulation that the custom of playing interludes, between each two stanzas of a hymn, has of late years fallen into comparative disuse among our best organists; and that at present, when an interlude is introduced by them, it is not for the mere purpose of display, but for a definite reason which may justify its use. Let us then consider the conditions under which interludes may be least objectionable, and, secondly, the best mode of their technical construction.

First condi-
tion under
which they
may be intro-
duced.
The first and most valid excuse for introducing an interlude, is that it gives the choir an opportunity to take breath.

This may be a legitimate reason in case of a *quartet* choir, to whom is given the task of singing five or six verses of a plain choral tune of the "Old Hundredth" pattern. It is not generally known by those utterly opposed to interludes under any circumstances, that it is far more fatiguing to sing a simple tune of the above class five or six times without pause, than to execute many a long anthem. Such tunes have to be sung with full voice, and not often can more than four syllables be sung to one breath. Thus, the immediate repetition for the above number of times would be really a great tax upon four voices. With a large chorus choir, this objection measurably (but not entirely) disappears, as the individual singer does not or need not tax his or her vocal powers to the same extent.

Even in the case previously assumed, there is no necessity of inserting an interlude after *each* verse. One is usually sufficient, and two as a maximum.

The height of the ridiculous is reached when an interlude is introduced between verses the first of which does not complete the idea, but leads directly to the following verse. As for instance :

> " We are his people, we his care,
> Our souls and all our mortal frame ;
> What lasting honors shall we rear,
> Almighty Maker, to thy name ?"

> " We'll crowd thy gates with thankful songs," etc.

To have the question of the first stanza conclude with the tonic chord of a common tune is bad enough ; for, as we have already seen (see remarks under Example 28, Chapter IV.), the complete cadence is diametrically opposed to the continuance of a thought expressed by words. To give this truly would require the half cadence. Thus, the common hymn-tune frequently brings with it discrepancies like the following. We take as an illustration the last strain of Example 6 :

EXAMPLE 120.

Al - migh - ty Mak - er, to thy name? to thy name ?

The music destroys the question. To give this properly would require the ending as at *b*. This would lead back immediately to a repetition of the tune. But hymnody is—hymnody. We can not afford to be too particular in all cases of this kind. Considering, however, that the musical phrase is itself defective as an interpretation of the text, it is equivalent to adding insult to injury when we respond to the question,

> " What lasting honors shall we rear,
> Almighty Maker, to thy name ?"

with *any* interlude, much more with an *average* one. It is evident that the immediate commencement of the following stanza is absolutely demanded in cases similar to the above.

Another condition under which an interlude may occasionally be introduced with propriety seems to be the following.

When the character of words radically changes, as regards sentiment, towards the close of a hymn, the interlude may be appropriately introduced as intermediating between the verses where such change occurs. The following stanzas illustrate a change of this character:

"Saviour, when night involves the skies,
My soul, adoring, turns to thee;
Thee, self-abased in mortal guise,
And wrapt in shades of death for me.

"On thee my waking raptures dwell
When crimson gleams the east adorn,
Thee, victor of the grave and hell,
Thee, source of life's eternal morn.

"When noon her throne in light arrays,
To thee my soul triumphant springs;
Thee, throned in glory's endless blaze
Thee, Lord of lords, and King of kings.

"O'er earth, when shades of evening steal,
To death and thee my thoughts I give;
To death, whose power I soon must feel,
To thee, with whom I trust to live."

Points of Introduction. That the natural sentiment of the second and third stanzas requires the tune chosen to be sung *forte*, if not *fortissimo*, and in a prompt, energetic manner, is evident. Equally so is the fact that the first and last stanzas require an opposite treatment. A short, well-constructed interlude can not here offend the requirements of good taste, if it seems to mitigate possible abruptness of style in passing from the triumph of verses 2 and 3 to the pensive tone of the last stanza. The opposite treatment might be employed between verses 1 and 2, in order to introduce the *forte* of verse 2. This is not in so good keeping as the introduction of the interlude after verse 3, as the tune has been heard but once.

Simplest form of Interlude when musical invention proves lacking. It is unfortunately true that a person may have a keen perception of the æsthetic requirements as above demanded, and yet be unable to express them in any fitting musical manner. This simply amounts to another argument against the use of extempore interludes by unqualified performers. Where interludes seem to be required (as, for instance, when a moment's breathing-time is to be given the choir), such persons have at least four simple sources from which to draw the necessary material. These are the four separate strains which constitute every long, common, or short metre tune. Of these four, the last is evidently the best, as it may be repeated literally. Its modulatory progress, if it have any, will be towards the tonic close, which forms at the same time the tonic opening for the repetition of the tune.

The three remaining strains may contain some modulatory tendency, probably in the direction of the dominant.* To avoid this, and yet to use the material which the strain offers and return to the tonic instead, will only require the change of a chord or two. This can be accomplished with but a slight knowledge of harmony.

Books or "Collections" of Interludes. The objection to the use of books or "collections" of interludes, designed for those who feel themselves incompetent to construct them for themselves, lies principally in the fact that a

---

* Of the manner in which such a modulation may be made available we shall speak later, page 124.

proper choice and adaptation of the same is apt to prove a failure. Outside the fact of the (usually) exceedingly poor musical quality of the interludes thus offered, they very rarely have any æsthetic relationship to the tune chosen. The inappropriateness of playing a little piece between the verses foreign in style to the hymn selected, and having nothing in common with it but the key of the piece, needs no comment.

Recognizing, then, the fact that interludes must or may be occasionally introduced, let us consider whence they may be derived, and some points of their technical construction, necessarily assuming that the pupil has some invention of his own and sufficient harmonic knowledge.

As regards style or character, the first source from which the interlude may be derived is Sources from the sentiment of the *succeeding* verse. The justice of this principle should be sufficiently clear from the comments upon the hymn previously quoted. As to its technical nature, it may be treated in three or four parts, contrapuntally or melodically, or as a solo upon one manual accompanied upon another. which the
Style of a
given Inter-
lude may be
derived.

As to its length, it is safe to say that it should never exceed eight bars in common measure. Length. The following example has but six, and illustrates the solo form :

EXAMPLE 121.

Let us suppose this interlude to be used to introduce the *last* verse of the hymn, " Saviour, when night involves the skies," which we may further suppose set to any appropriate tune in the key of C. This simple interlude leads to the following comments :

The third verse of the hymn ending in a triumphant vein, the interlude begins *mezzo-forte*, Influence of and at a comparatively high compass. With the third measure, the *diminuendo* begins and continues to the close, introducing the pensive tone of the last stanza. To further this purpose, it will be noticed that the melody of the interlude gradually descends in compass, until it reaches the tonic more than an octave below the point it started from. Besides this, the " flats" introduced belong properly to the key of C minor, and at once lend a sombre coloring to the close. The *sense* of being in the key of C minor is not so firmly established, however, but that the interlude may be satisfactorily concluded, and the following verse naturally begun in the key of C major. Besides this, as far as tonality is concerned, we know that any composition in minor may close with the major instead of the minor tonic chord. Still, different shades of expression Shades of Ex- may be obtained by varying the number of flats introduced in Example 121. Compass, Di-
minuendo,
and Minor
Chords as
means of ac-
complishing
change of
sentiment.

pression.

Let the student test this by playing the phrase first as given, then with the E flat omitted (in both melody and accompaniment), then omitting the A flat and E flat, and finally omitting all the flats given.

In so doing, he should keep ever in view that the object to be attained is not what he may deem the happiest melodic effect considered by itself, but that best suited to introduce the final stanza of this particular hymn.

The three
Elements em-
ployed in pre-
ceding exam-
ple not obli-
gatory.
Three elements, then, lend their aid in gradually introducing the changed sentiment of the stanza referred to—namely: (1) *descending compass*, (2) *diminished power*, and (3) the *introduction of special minor intervals within the major key.*

The above remarks (as in many instances in this work) are given simply as a hint to the student, but in no sense as an obligatory formula to which he should necessarily confine himself, even under precisely similar conditions.

Example
without dy-
namic change,
and with
ascending
compass.
Even in the case cited, the interlude *might* contain no diminution of power, no descending compass, and no marked leading towards the minor key. In such a case, however, the interlude *would* require to be held "piano" throughout, if it be intended to meet the sentiment of the following verse. An example of this kind follows, which, we think, will not be found inappropriate to this specific case.

EXAMPLE 122.

Here there is no decrescendo, no tendency of a decided character towards the minor key, and the general direction of the compass is upward.

Beginning in
Minor at
once.
For a similar change of sentiment, a fitting interlude may also be constructed by beginning in minor at once. In such case, the return to the major key must be made early enough to insure the sense of tonality, which the voices require in order to begin the following verse— perhaps somewhat after the following manner:

EXAMPLE 123.

Use of "re-
mote" Modu-
lation.
A word or two may be said here in regard to the use of remote modulation in an interlude. Such modulation is not absolutely to be prohibited, but it is dangerous except under the hands of a master. Its tendency is to spin out the interlude to an undue length, and he who attempts it should have some given motive for introducing it, and should, furthermore, have the whole harmonic system at easy command. He should also be able to compress such unusual effects into the ordinary scope of an interlude, and, within that limit, must lead away from and back to the key of the piece without doing violence to the singer's sense of tonality. He who attempts this without the presupposed qualification is tolerably certain—to use a common phrase —of "coming to grief." This expression is particularly applicable here, as it describes not only the result as it affects the player, but also the sensations of those who listen to him. We will risk giving one example of this class without precisely recommending its imitation. The student should previously play over some tune of a quiet character in the key of F, ¾, so as to well establish the tonality.

EXAMPLE 124.

In all the remarks that have thus far been made in regard to the construction of interludes, we shall have failed in our purpose if we have not made evident to the reader the one thought which should underlie the whole—to wit: that he who would extemporize an interlude should have a definite musical and æsthetic purpose in so doing. The mere breathing opportunity for the voices is not enough. A given mood should be depicted, a given situation portrayed, if possible. *Definite purpose.*

Among the disturbing influences which an inexperienced player may create in extemporizing an interlude, is that of uncertainty of rhythm. Outside of change of *tempo* (which may sometimes be permitted), change of *measure* during the interlude will often produce a disturbing effect. Thus, it is by no means of so rare occurrence to hear a tune in common measure ($\frac{4}{4}$) followed by an interlude in triple measure ($\frac{3}{4}$). *Uncertainty of Rhythm.*

Recurring to Example 121, the student should note the opening of the interlude, as beginning with an incomplete part of the measure—thus: etc. *Beginning with incomplete measure.*

This manner of beginning the interlude is especially useful when a solo-stop is to be employed, and when at the same time the interlude is to be of a quiet character. It enables the organist to avoid absolutely any break between the close of the tune and the beginning of the interlude.

EXAMPLE 125.

Thee, Lord of lords and King of kings.

Supposing the tune to end *forte* as at *a*, the organist can play the ending as at *b*. Here it is seen that the interlude is begun before the voices cease, the organ first really asserting itself in the following measure. This prevents the break above alluded to.

Attention is also called to the fact of the prolongation of the pedal tone at the close of the tune (Example 125, *b*) after the organist has removed his hands from the last chord of the accompaniment. This prolongation of course implies the withdrawal of the Great to Pedal Coupler. *Prolonging Pedal Tone.*

Occasional retaining the Break between Tune and Interlude. On the other hand, in interludes of a jubilant character with a strong registration (for instance, the Full Swell), the break between verse and interlude may be made evident, and treated as a part of the musical effect. Thus, many forms similar to the following example may be employed in which the "eighth-rest" introduces the interlude after the voices have ceased. In this instance, the rhythmic effect which the rest produces is continued imitatively throughout, thus giving the interlude a certain unity of design.

EXAMPLE 126.

Use of dominant Cadence as a means of closing Interlude and beginning the Tune. In the majority of instances, a close connection between tune and interlude is preferable. The desire to accomplish this sometimes prompts the better harmonists among our church-players to give the interlude some other form of close than that of the complete cadence in the tonic—in other words, to construct the interlude in such a way that its close *creates an expectancy of the tonic chord*, which chord is immediately supplied by the re-entrance of the voices. The expert harmonist can accomplish this in many ways, but the underlying principle which governs all the varied forms will always be that of the "half," or "dominant" cadence.

Choice of Harmonies as leading to Tone with which the Soprano part begins. The choice of these means, and the various inversions employed, should depend largely upon the particular interval of the chord *with which the Sopranos commence the tune*. Experience shows that in an interlude of this class, where the tune follows without break, it is safer so to construct it that the Soprano may, so to speak, hear her tone coming, or realize what it is to be. This is because the Soprano carries the melody, and the prompt entrance of the melody is all-important.

A few illustrations will exemplify the truth of the above; and, to avoid any possible misunderstanding, we state the required conditions once more.

It is desired to construct an interlude, which, at its close, shall avoid the complete cadence to the tonic; transferring the same to the opening of the tune itself. Furthermore, the interlude is to be so constructed that it shall, in an especial manner, give the Soprano voices their pitch for the opening chord of the tune.

EXAMPLE 127.

EXAMPLE 128.

Forms similar to the above might be multiplied *ad libitum*, but the six examples given contain the essence of the principle advocated. This the student should seek to apply in other ways and in varied keys.

When the "half" instead of the complete cadence is employed to end an interlude, it becomes very important that the singers *listen*, in order to begin the tune promptly. No trouble need be experienced if an organist will but call his choir's attention once or twice to this manner of introducing the tune.

"Motion" in the Interlude as compared with the tune.

It may have been noticed that a number of the examples previously given in this chapter conclude with a slight *ritardando*. This is owing to the quicker *motion* given the interlude, but not necessarily quicker *tempo*. That is, when the tune is written in half notes, the prevailing notation of the interlude may, with advantage, be given in quarters. If the tune be written in quarters, the motion may be in eighths. Thus, the *ritardando* mediates between the interlude as a whole and the resumption of the tune in simpler rhythm. The relation of half notes to eighths will sometimes, but rarely, occur. When employed, the tempo should be moderate, and it should be chiefly introduced in interludes of a joyous character. Even then, the eighth-note motion is preferable in the bass rather than in the upper voice. Otherwise, the interlude is apt to become too florid, and out of keeping with a church service.

"Thematic Treatment."

We now proceed to consider another means by which interludes may be constructed, and one which demands of the organist considerably greater artistic qualifications than the construction of the forms thus far given.

We refer to what is termed " thematic treatment." This is the great source of development of large compositions from small germs or "motives," and requires long-continued studies in composition proper. As it exceeds the theoretic knowledge demanded of the pupil (in the preliminary requirements stated at the beginning of this work), it can not be expected that a treatise on the subject should be introduced here. In the first place, the interlude is *not* a large composition, nor does it require development in the sense stated. On the contrary, it needs the utmost possible condensation of thought. Notwithstanding this, thematic treatment proves, even here, of such eminent value that we venture to introduce a few examples, and say a few words as to its possible application for our purpose. May it attract the student to the study of this most important branch of musical theory, or, at least, give him some idea of the possibilities of its application.

Application where no change of sentiment occurs in the words chosen.

We have seen that the character of an interlude may be derived from the *following* stanza of a hymn, a given verse of which has just been sung.

This was justified more especially by an approaching change of sentiment.

Now, in many cases where an interlude may be desired, we have no particularly marked change of sentiment. Besides this, we have metrical versions of the Psalms (not to speak of other so-called sacred "poetry") which are so didactic in character, with so slight, if any, vestige of the lyrical element which music requires, that a plain choral tune is about the only adaptation to which they can be set. Among these (chorales) there is frequently no particular choice as to

Sentiment of Verses which can not be expressed in Music.

which is selected. Thus, the following verse, which is to be found in many of our hymn-books, would scarcely excite the invention, not to say inspiration, of the most expert organist:

> " The hand that gave it still supplies
> The gracious light and heat ;
> His truths upon the nations rise,
> They rise, and never set !"

And this by no less a poet than Cowper! In such cases, the (qualified) organist can " fly for refuge " to the thematic treatment of motives derived from the tune sung.*

---

* It is not to be understood that thematic treatment is to be *confined* to such conditions as the above ; nor that it is only to be used as a last resource. It has its own intrinsic value, and is not simply a mechanical resort, or technical means of evading a difficulty. It can, under proper conditions, express feeling or sentiment as truly as if the player were not confined to a given " motive." To well accomplish a musical result, within bounds which a musician sets himself voluntarily, is art, even in so insignificant a thing as an Interlude.

To illustrate this as simply as may be, we recur to our former Example 14, giving, for brevity's sake, only the melody, and in the modern (quarter-note) notation.

"London-New."

Thou art the way, to thee a-lone From sin and death we flee ; And he who would the Father seek, Must seek him.Lord, by thee.

These words are worthy of being called sacred poetry, but they contain a theological proposition—nothing with which music has any thing in common. The remaining verses are virtually of the same character. But it is to be sung! Therefore, for a musical setting, we turn to a plain choral tune—dignified, indeed, in style, but containing no marked characteristics which would hinder it from being used for hundreds of other and similar hymns. For a similar reason we turn for material for our interlude to thematic treatment and the tune itself.

A "motive" taken from a tune is—to put it familiarly—a "bit" of the tune itself, taking more or less of it according to the development desired. It is self-evident that no motive can consist of *less* than two notes. Careful examination of the choral theme given shows that it is

What constitutes a "Thematic Motive."

made up largely from the following thematic bits—namely :  being in the one case the skip of a fifth, in the other that of a fourth. We find other skips of thirds and sixths (G—B♭, G—E♭), as well as progressions by degree, but we think the student can not but perceive that they arise by way of simple imitation and variation of the first two notes. At all events, we select these first two notes (see above at *a*) as the short "motive," out of which to develop an interlude thematically by means of simple "imitation."

EXAMPLE 133.

Within the scope of four Measures.

This is thematic treatment in its simplest form, and made almost exclusively through imitation of the skips of fifths and fourths contained in the tune itself. The bass happens here to bring the identical notes of the second strain of the chorale, the last measure but one being in augmented values.

Should a longer interlude be desired, a half cadence, introduced in place of the previous complete cadence, will carry us further—thus :

Development by postponing tonic Cadence.

EXAMPLE 134.

Unity of Thought. The student should very carefully compare Example 134 with the choral melody, in order to fully realize the fact that no new material is introduced. The intimate musical relation thus established between tune and interlude will be evident, for the thoughts offered are the same as those contained in the tune, but clothed in another dress—viewed in another light. Thus, the interlude is of the same musical essence as the tune, and the result is musical unity.

It is not to be forgotten that we may *not* desire unity of musical thought, as in case of a radical change of sentiment in the words. In such case, we have no need to have recourse to the thematic mode of constructing interludes.

Treatment by means of repeating a whole strain. Another (and freer) species of thematic treatment occurs when, instead of a couple of tones, we take a whole strain of the original chorale to be treated as an interlude. In the example which follows, we take the last strain for this purpose:

EXAMPLE 135.

Change of Harmonies upon repetition. By comparison with the tune, it will be perceived that the last strain is repeated three times, the last time in the tenor. In the literal repetition of such short phrases, the principal thing to observe (besides preserving the harmonic motion when once established) is the change of harmonies with each repetition of the strain. Thus the skip  is first harmonized afterwards and finally

Another mode of treatment. Another form of interlude which can not be termed "thematic," but yet is somewhat akin to it, consists in the repetition of a couple of strains; literally as to melody, with other harmonizations; and, perhaps, a florid contrapuntal figure accompanying it. This form is especially effective if the choral theme is put in the tenor range with comparatively strong registration. The following example treats the first two strains of the tune:

EXAMPLE 136.

Recapitulation. The several sources from which we may draw material for interludes should now be sufficiently evident to the pupil. Let us, before proceeding further, briefly recapitulate them. We have, first, the free interlude which employs melodies and harmonies *not* derived from the tune itself; secondly, the thematic interlude constructed from "motives" of the tune;

thirdly, the employment of a strain or two of the choral theme, varied as to its harmony, or with the addition of a free contrapuntal part. This we have illustrated in Example 136.

The free form finds its most natural employment when a decided change of sentiment is to be expressed. This change of sentiment goes far towards justifying the introduction of new musical material foreign to the original tune.

The thematic form is especially available when the sentiment does not change, and its employment preserves musical unity of thought where the organist would not otherwise know *what* to express in his interlude.

It only remains for us to speak of the possible union of these two forms (changing sentiment and thematic treatment) in one and the same interlude. This, in many cases, is not so difficult for a good harmonist who possesses some invention. The problem, then, be it understood, is this: on the one hand, to construct an interlude which shall form the appropriate link between two verses of widely varying sentiment. On the other, to construct such an interlude solely from thematic material derived from the tune itself. The following example attempts to illustrate a union of this kind. We again take the hymn, "Saviour, when night involves the skies," the purpose being to lead from the sentiment of the third to that of the last stanza, introducing the same by a half cadence, so that the voices may enter upon the tonic. We set the words to the tune given, as Example 47, to which the student should refer for its harmonic character.

Treatment of change of sentiment by thematic means.

When noon her throne in light ar - rays, To thee my soul tri - umph - ant springs;

Thee, throned in glo - ry's end - less blaze, Thee, Lord of lords and King of kings.

The student has here a good example of simple thematic treatment as applied to the construction of the *theme itself*—the whole tune being constructed out of the slight material offered in the first measure, the necessary cadences excepted. Keeping, then, in mind the above sentiment, and that the last stanza (see page 120) begins "O'er earth, when shades of evening steal," etc., the interlude might proceed as follows:

Thematic origin of the theme itself.

EXAMPLE 137.

The thematic motive is given in large notes, in order that the student may everywhere recognize its employment.

Objection which may be raised against the examples here given.

To the young organist who is desirous of extemporizing his interludes, the following objection or criticism may occur, applicable to all the examples given in this chapter. "It is all very well for the author," we can imagine him saying, "to write out these interludes as illustrations of the doctrine he is advocating. He can deliberately design them, put them on paper, alter, and remould them to suit his purpose. I can not think of all these points of construction, etc., when an interlude is suddenly demanded of me in church." Such comments would imply a far higher compliment to the specimens given than they deserve. A great talent is not necessary to *extemporize* examples fully as good as those given, but a knowledge of treatment and some practical experience *are* required.

He who would extemporize interludes must be theoretically competent.

It is true that the player can not be thinking of rules, nor is it required. It is, nevertheless, an absolute necessity that he who would aspire to play a good interlude must unconsciously be governed by these very laws. He must have previously recognized their force, and digested the ideas involved in their execution. Thus, the workings of his mind in regard to them are the same as in case of the literary workman in regard to the rules of grammar—namely : a controlling force, of which he is practically unconscious at the very time he is applying the principles they involve. The student may rest assured that, to justify his playing extempore interludes at all, he should be able to construct, offhand, similar forms to those given.

We have dwelt upon this subject at some length, that we might, if possible, impress upon the minds of those interested in this matter the possibility of giving interludes a definite purpose, and thus avoid the empty, meaningless wanderings over the keys which we are so frequently called upon to endure in our churches. Even the organist naturally possessing plenty of musical invention requires to be guided by the laws of musical construction. This chapter will not have been written in vain if it lead students to make themselves familiar with these laws ; neither will it have been written in vain if it bring to those who have no inventive gift nor theoretical knowledge such a perception of what is actually required to produce an acceptable interlude, *that they cease to attempt it.* Such persons (as we have before indicated, page 120) should confine themselves to repeating one of the strains of the tune sung.

The *Writing* of Interludes as a preliminary to extempore performance.

The young organist who is studying music as a profession, or any of our gifted amateurs who may have the privilege of an extended course of theoretical instruction, will find it a most useful exercise to *write out* interludes to given tunes. By so doing, and by striving to give the interlude a meaning of its own, they will greatly strengthen their powers in this direction. It will be found the best preparation for extemporizing interludes which shall not be destitute of "form and void." The less frequently interludes are introduced the better. This being the case, such as are introduced should be musically and æsthetically worthy.

CHAPTER XII.

THE organist who always plays the notes simply *as written* (in pieces requiring the use of eight-foot stops only), loses sight of a means of accompaniment which, in given cases, may prove of much value. This is the exceptional use of the stops.

Most organ-registers, if examined tone by tone, will be found to have a " best range," where their quality is most individual, although their compass may extend throughout the keyboard.

Now, if we play in chords, making use of these stops singly, at a range which is relatively too high or too low for their best qualities, we obtain an effect either too piercing or too thick and muffled in character, as the case may be.

Again, the pupil has seen in Chapter I. that the various lengths of the pipes produce many duplicates of the same tone. Thus, the following three phrases,

EXAMPLE 138.

will be found to be identical with each other in pitch when played alternately with the stops indicated, and with such only. Both the phrases at *b* (four feet) and at *c* (sixteen feet) will sound the tones represented by the phrase at *a* (eight feet) in actual unison.

The same practical test at the instrument, while showing this identity of pitch, reveals a more or less marked discrepancy as to quality or character of tone, and sometimes as to power. This discrepancy will vary in different instruments, and must therefore be sought out by the player, and the various stops compared with each other in the respect indicated.

The following remarks may serve to indicate to the student the general manner in which he may pursue this examination, and the practical use which may be derived from such differences in quality. Bearing in mind the variations in degree which various stops of various organs exhibit, it will be found, as a general rule, that a stop of low pitch (sixteen feet), when played in chords an octave higher than written, gives a larger and frequently more mellow tone than a stop of eight feet played as written. The tone does not necessarily change in power, but rather in quality. It is to be premised that the same notes are played in each case, the difference lying only in the octave touched by the fingers.

On the other hand, a stop of four feet, played in chords an octave lower than written, gives a tone of less fulness than the eight-foot stop played as written, although in quality it may be brighter or more sparkling.

Comparisons instituted between Stops of the same Manual.

It should be understood that comparisons of the kind to which we refer apply only to stops of a given manual, and not to any two stops of different manuals. This is because the relative balance of single stops is only fairly to be judged by their relation to the remaining stops of the manual to which they themselves belong. Furthermore, such comparisons should, at first, be only instituted between stops of a similar nature—that is, comparing metal pipes with metal, wood with wood, etc. Thus, the Open.Diapason (metal) of sixteen feet may be compared with the Open Diapason of eight feet, and the Principal or Octave of four feet by transposition in the octave above and below. The same may be done with the string-toned stops of the Swell and Choir Organs. Even the smaller instruments are now usually provided with a string-toned stop of eight feet and one of four feet in the Swell (Salicional or Keraulophon and Violin). The Great Organ rarely has a string-toned stop of either sixteen or four feet, except in the largest instruments.

Differences sufficient to modify effects.

Slight as these differences may prove in a given instrument, they are sufficiently marked in most cases to afford the player just the slight modification of effect, in simple accompaniments, which he may desire, and which the normal use of the stops may not give him.

After the comparison of stops of varying lengths, but of similar character, has received due attention, the student may proceed to examine the shades of difference between comparatively unrelated stops, testing them by the same transpositions. This may be accomplished by short progressions, somewhat after the following manner:

EXAMPLE 139.

Dulc. 8ft.   Flute, 4ft.   15th, or Piccolo.

Practical application in Accompaniment.

The explanation of these differences lies chiefly in the varying scales (dimensions) of the pipes, comprising the various stops of similar or of contrasting tone. Their practical application in accompaniment will be found principally in solo work, or at least in passages where but few voices are employed. There will rarely be any thing gained in comparing an Open Diapason of sixteen feet with one of eight feet, as the discrepancy in voicing will usually be too slight, but among the softer stops, and especially among the family of Flutes, good results may often be obtained. Thus, supposing a solo or recitative (of considerably greater length than the following example) to be continuously accompanied in chords, lying rather high, after the following manner:

EXAMPLE 140.

Sop'r Solo.   MENDELSSOHN.

My God, with - in me is my soul cast   down!   etc.

4ft. 8va lower.   8ft.   etc.

If a four-foot Flute be employed, instead of a Melodia or Stopped Diapason, playing the Transposi-tion in the lower Octave. chord (Example 140) an octave lower, a tone of perhaps less fulness (especially as compared with the Melodia), but of greater brightness (especially as compared with the Stopped Diapason), will be obtained. This may, under conditions, better agree with the voice accompanied, or the contrary effect may result therefrom.

It is evident that such treatment becomes a matter of judgment and experiment on the part of the organist. It is also evident that this kind of transposition in the octave must be confined to accompaniments of limited compass, as they would otherwise pass beyond the range of the keyboard when so transposed, and, should but a single key be lacking, the phrase might thereby be mutilated. This use of the stops is, however, by no means confined to a limited range of Transposi-tion in the upper Octave. chords, but may often advantageously be employed for many passages founded upon the scales.

EXAMPLE 141.

At *a*, Example 141, the bass passage is given as written for the piano. This, it will be seen, descends below the manual compass of the organ. It may, notwithstanding, be literally executed by the employment of two manuals—registering the right hand with eight-foot stops, and the left with the Great Open Diapason (or Bourdon) of sixteen feet, and playing the bass an octave higher than written. Should special distinctness be desired in the bass, an eight-foot stop may be added to the sixteen-foot, thus giving the passage in octaves. In this way, many pedal passages may be performed, where not too great power is required, which might otherwise be found to exceed the clear and comfortable execution of the player. Instances also occur when transposition to the lower octave with eight-foot stops produces the best effect.*

At *b*, Example 141, compare the effect of the ascending passage played as written with the Choir (or Great Organ) Melodia, and the same played an octave lower with the Flute of four feet. It must be remembered that an effect not exceeding *mezzo-piano* is desired.

If the Pedal Organ is large, and provided with stops of eight and even of four feet, a Eight- and four-foot use of the Pedals in giving out a theme. choral melody may sometimes be given to the pedals, while the real (fundamental) bass is executed by the left hand upon the manual with sixteen- and eight-foot stops ; the sixteen-foot tone being omitted from the pedals. Taking our former example, No. 57, as a theme, the form proposed would be as follows :†

EXAMPLE 142.

* See Chapter IV., page 30, on "Employment of eight-foot Manual-stops in the lower octave instead of the Pedal."

† In this connection, the student should also refer carefully to the reading matter given with Example 57.

It will be noticed that (the Pedal having no sixteen-foot stops drawn) the theme is given out as a *Cantus Firmus* in the Tenor. In this respect, it is identical with Example 57 itself. Due consideration of the condition as exhibited in Example 142 will show, however, that wholly different effects of registration are here attainable. In Example 57, the left hand was confined to the principal manual and the theme itself. Here both hands are free to execute the *accompaniment* upon two manuals, with contrasting registration, if desired. If the Pedal Organ is powerful enough by itself, and if a three-manual organ should chance to be at the disposal of the performer, he has then three manuals from which to draw effects in registration, leaving to the Pedal alone the duty of supporting the theme. If the Pedal is not sufficiently powerful in stops of eight and four feet, he can couple with the Swell reeds or other stops of eight and four feet. There will still remain to him two manuals for purposes of registration. If the organ

Pedal eight-
foot effect
through
coupling. possess but two manuals, he must either rely upon the Pedal Organ alone for giving the theme prominence—in which case a soft accompanimental registration may be employed—or he may couple with that manual which has no sixteen-foot stop drawn. This is also the way to be employed when the organ possesses no eight-foot pedal-stop. In such case, the effect is only to be obtained, if at all, through coupling. The use of the pedals, then, becomes a purely mechanical one, as they utter no tone of their own, but simply free the hands for other purposes.

This treatment is by no means recommended as a form to be employed off-hand, when giving out the tune from the book, but to be maturely considered by the student as a means of registration, and possibly written out by him as an exercise.

An example of far more elaborate character coming under this head is offered in the Variations by Rink on "God save the King" (Variation 8). We give but two measures, as the work itself is well known among organists and easily procurable:

EXAMPLE 143.

It will be seen that the registration (by W. T. Best) calls for a pedal reed of four feet. This will not only give the *Cantus Firmus* a decided prominence, but it will also cause the theme to be heard in tenor range *above* the contrapuntal bass as played by the left hand. It is scarcely possible to perform this variation without a stop of this kind in the Pedal Organ, on account of the upward range of the choral theme, which precludes its being played an octave higher with eight-foot stops.

Transposition
of Pedal-part
in the upper
Octave. It not unfrequently occurs that the principle of transposition in the upper octave may be advantageously applied to the sixteen-foot stops of the Pedal Organ, when the compass allows of such transposition. This finds its most frequent use when a light pedal bass, of equal fulness, but of less positiveness than the lower notes of the Violoncello, eight feet, is required. The Violoncello consisting of open metal and the Bourdon of stopped wooden pipes, the lower end of the former will naturally have a more incisive tone than the upper notes of the latter. As the Bourdon speaks an octave lower than written, the pitch will not be changed by the mere mechanical transposition of the passage.

By means of this treatment, in such organs as do not possess a Pedal Flute of eight feet (a most useful stop), a tolerable makeshift for the same can be obtained from the upper notes of the Bourdon, providing that the stop is a good one. Organists who may test this should not be satisfied with listening to this stop at the keys, but try it (by the aid of another performer) at a distance and in different parts of the church.

The "stopping" of the Bourdon pipes (with a wooden plug) causes them sometimes to sound a harmonic, usually the fifth, in connection with their fundamental tone, the harmonic being at times unpleasantly distinct. This same cause, together with the manner in which these pipes are usually placed within the organ—on opposite sides and to the rear of the instrument—may lead the player to consider the voicing defective, when judging it at the keys. Of two adjoining tones, one may appear too strong and one too weak, not to speak of variations in quality. If the stop is well made, he will find that these apparent defects—both as to balance and as to the harmonics—will disappear when heard at a proper distance.

Characteristics of the Pedal Bourdon.

The use of the Bourdon in the upper octave (uncoupled) proves especially useful when it is desired to have the actual bass tone lie near the harmony. This, on account of a more intimate blending of the parts, with which, if played in the lower octave, it would not readily unite itself. By returning to the lower octave, at the same time coupling with the Swell or Choir Organ, the effect of a sixteen-foot stop is produced.

The following example (from the Septuor of Beethoven, transcribed for the organ) illustrates such a transposition in the octave.

EXAMPLE 144.

N.B.—Bourdon 16ft. only, uncoupled.

At *a*, the pedal gives the tone of an eight-foot stop, played an octave lower, and is thus identical with the low A of the Violoncello. Were the Bourdon employed in the lower octave, the actual tone would be [notation] two octaves distant from the nearest manual tone. The student should regard the above example, at *a*, from the standpoint of simple accompaniment, viewing the Clarionet Solo as a vocal one.

At *b*, the *melody* being given in a higher octave, a *lower bass* is required. The Bourdon descends to the lower octave, where it first may be said to assert its definite sixteen-foot character. Distinctness of tone enunciation in the Bass is provided for by the pedals having been previously coupled to the Swell, which is registered with eight-foot stops.

Of the "First and Second Octave" in the Pedal Open Diapason.

This treatment can rarely be resorted to in case of the Pedal Open Diapason of sixteen feet, on account of the large scale of its pipes, and the radical quality of its tone in the second octave.

It is none the less true, however, that the second octave may be preferable, in many cases requiring, at least, a *mezzo-forte* bass, where but few voices are singing, and where a definite but strong foundation is required. By *definite* foundation, we understand a tone the pitch of which is easily determined by the ear in its relation to the voices. This is not the case with the low pedal tones, unless they form the foundation to quite a powerful combination involving the use of stops of high pitch. The student may, perhaps, best appreciate this, by comparing with each other the relative qualities of tone between 𝄢 and 𝄢 with the chromatic intervals; the Pedal Open Diapason, of sixteen feet, only being drawn. That the lower octave of this stop is far too frequently used in accompaniment by the majority of organists is certain.[*] Even when necessarily thus employed, a change from the lower to the upper octave gives variety of effect. In the latter case, the obligato form of pedal-playing should be made use of, the left hand playing the Tenor part (in four-part harmony), and leaving the Bass to the pedals. When the lower octave is employed, the left hand may duplicate the Bass in the upper octave upon the manual, or supply fuller harmonies if necessary.

Omission of eight-foot Tone.

We have seen that the fundamental principle of registration consists in the predominance of the eight-foot tone. An exception to this is sometimes made in *solo-playing*, where a peculiar brilliance of effect is desired, by omitting the eight-foot tone entirely, and substituting two stops, one of sixteen and the other of four feet. The tones thus produced are necessarily two octaves apart.

Meantime, the accompaniment is played upon another manual with a soft eight foot registration. Thus the accompaniment really occupies the middle ground, as to pitch, between the two. The general rule is not entirely set aside, except so far as the eight-foot tone does not predominate. It still serves to call special attention to the peculiar distance from each other occupied by the solo-stops for a peculiar purpose. In such a combination, the passage must not run too low, as the sixteen-foot stop would then render it too gloomy.

Stops of eight and two feet, without those of four feet.

A somewhat similar and still brighter effect may be produced by combining stops of eight and two feet to the omission of all four-foot stops. The accompaniment differs here from the former instance, in that it does not supply the missing interval—namely, the four-foot stops— but must still retain an essentially eight-foot registration. The Clarionet of the Choir Organ lends itself particularly well to this effect, as the lower stop of the solo combination, using the Piccolo or (in default of it) the Fifteenth for the upper tone.

Conditions of use with voices.

If the above combinations are to be sparingly introduced in solo-playing, the same holds good to a still more decided extent in accompanying voices. It may occur, however, that just this peculiarity of effect may be desirable for a short time, by way of contrast; or it may be desired to make prominent a certain figuration of the accompaniment for a certain number of measures, as an essential characteristic of the piece. Where many dissonances occur in the figuration between voices and accompaniment, they are felt far more in case of the organ than when they are produced by either piano or orchestra. In such cases, this exceptional registration may find

---

* See remarks on "Pedal abuse," Chap. IV., page 30.

use. An example follows of the possible employment of stops of sixteen and four feet, to the exclusion of those of eight feet:

EXAMPLE 145.

We remark, at first, that, although the G clef is here conventionally used for the Tenor and Bass voices, yet they actually sound an octave lower. This being noted, it will be seen at once that a strong eight-foot registration of the accompanimental figure would cross in and out among the voices, tending to disturb them and blur a clear vocal performance. If the passage were given to Sopranos and Altos, this criticism would not hold good, as the vocal parts would then sound an octave higher. As it is, however, the male voices *do represent the eight-foot pitch.* Relation of Accompaniment to male voices in a given case.

Let us now suppose the instrumental Bass to be registered with the Great Organ Open Diapason (or Bourdon) of sixteen feet, and the Principal or Octave of four feet. In case the latter should be too strong, the Harmonic Flute of four feet may be strong enough. It must be borne in mind that the fingers execute the passage precisely as given in Example 145, but the sixteen-foot stop gives the octave lower than written, while that of four feet sounds an octave higher than written. The following example shows the effect in relation to the voices:

EXAMPLE 146.

This unusual treatment is only justified on the ground that the voices clearly predominate. The eight-foot
As voices, whether male or female, correspond in pitch with the eight-foot stops of the Pitch represented by the
organ, it will be seen that this registration is apparently rather than really exceptional, in so far voices as a
as it conflicts with the fundamental principle previously stated. In other words, the *voices* constituent
assume and clearly maintain the eight-foot pitch in lieu of the stops The small notes in part of the
Example 146 represent the part of the right hand in the accompaniment. The registration is combination.
eight feet, but is seen to bear a four-foot relation to the male voices.

The following is a parallel illustration for female voices with registration of eight and two feet—say Choir Clarionet and Piccolo. The voices are not duplicated by the accompaniment, as in the previous example.

EXAMPLE 147.

Use of eight and two foot stops with female voices.

Accompaniment in " Double Counterpoint of the Octave."

Choir to Great "Sub-octave" Coupler.

Contrasting Basses.

Motive which should prompt such treatment.

The Piccolo will here give the octave above the voices, as did similarly the Octave, four feet, in the previous example; the voices preserving the same relation as before—namely: lying between the octaves of the accompanying figuration. As a harmony in chords underlies this example, it does not devolve on the voices, in this instance, to create a realizing sense of eight-foot pitch, as in the previous illustration.

The expert harmonist will understand that where the accompaniment admits of such exceptional treatment as the above, it should be so constructed as to permit of the inversion of the figuration. This occurs through the repetition of such figuration in the octave above the voices, and must not thereby create false or forbidden intervals or progressions in its new relation to the voices. In other words, it must be written in Double Counterpoint.

Some three-manual organs contain a "Choir to Great Organ *sub-octave* coupler." By means of this, a number of charming special effects of this class may be obtained. When used as a solo, the right hand plays the upper notes upon the Great Organ, and the lower octave is mechanically obtained (by means of the coupler) from the Choir Organ. In this way, too, delicate sixteen-foot effects, of varying qualities, according to the combination, may be obtained by playing full chords in both hands upon the Great Organ.

Under the head of exceptional use of stops as applied to accompaniment, may also be classed the registration of basses (and sometimes other parts), with a different quality of tone from that employed to supply the remaining parts of the harmony. Special illustrations of this character are scarcely necessary, and may easily be discovered by the student. In making practical use of such basses, it should be for a purpose, and not simply for the sake of having one hand differently registered from another. Such contrasts will usually be made between the various Flutes and the reeds and string-toned stops—the two latter being preferable for such basses. They may also be contrasted with the Diapasons.

The motive which prompts such treatment should be found in some particularly significant melodic or harmonic progression in the part so registered, and which is thus made plain to the listener's perception by the peculiar registration.[*]

As a general rule, the Bass should agree in kind with the prevailing registration—as reeds with reed basses, flutes with flute or stopped diapason basses, etc. Mixtures alone may be said to have no exceptional use, and should be strictly confined to a powerful chorus accompaniment, either with or without reeds.

---

* See remarks following Example 26.

In concluding this chapter, the student should understand that the effects herein treated of are not, so to speak, of the every-day description, nor to be introduced at random. In some organs, they might sound badly, or at least disappoint his expectations. Of one thing, however, he may be positively certain: that such examinations into the relations of qualities of tone, among and between given stops, will result in a far more thorough acquaintance with the merits and demerits of the particular instrument with which he has to do than can be obtained in twice the time in any other way. This more than compensates for time expended in this direction, even if the student prefers to reject all exceptional effects after making the practical test.

If the general principles which govern the matter have been well mastered, the search for these same exceptional effects (of which comparatively few have been touched upon here) will bring him suddenly, as it were, to that which so many *blindly* seek, and therefore do *not* find— to wit: a competent knowledge of the Art of Registration.

CHAPTER XIII.

THE STACCATO TOUCH.

Effect of
mechanical
improvements
upon the use
of this Touch.
THE ability of the organ to sustain tone at the option of the player, renders it particularly well suited to compositions requiring the use of the legato touch and style. Notwithstanding this, the staccato touch, as applied to accompaniment, as well as to solo-playing, may frequently be made use of with the best results.

The great and general improvement in both voicing and mechanism, which has shown itself among our organ-builders of late years, has resulted in such an increased promptitude of " speech " from most of the pipes, that certain differences of touch may be permitted the performer of to-day, upon our modern organs, which it would be useless to attempt upon our older instruments. Besides the greater rapidity of execution now attainable, the possibility of getting a prompt staccato has been markedly affected by this change for the better.

Characteristics of the Organ Staccato as compared with the Piano.
Upon the piano we have two kinds of staccato, differing in degree—namely : and the former being much shorter and more sharply defined than the latter. Upon the piano this is easily accomplished, as every tone is produced by striking a key even in case of legato-playing. Upon the organ, the first kind of staccato given above is extremely rare. We have principally to do with the second species, and it is accomplished not so much by the blow of the finger upon the key as by a prompt " letting-go " of the same.

Modern Organ Touch other than Staccato.
It is a fact, however, that the promptness of speech of our modern organs, with the greatly increased execution demanded, admits, and even frequently requires, a touch more nearly approximating that of the piano than was formerly the case. This, too, applies not so much to any " blow " of the finger, as to the similarly prompt rise and fall of the fingers from the knuckle-joint, as in piano-playing.

This in contradistinction to the old " wiping " touch, with the finger slightly drawn-in upon the key, once so common with the old instruments and players.

Duration of Organ Staccato as compared with the Piano.
When we examine the staccato effects producible upon the organ, we find that they are most telling when treated as contrasts. As such, they should be of comparatively short duration, previous to and after which the legato touch should prevail.

Here the true nature of the instrument reveals itself ; for we have piano pieces which demand a continuous staccato from beginning to end. Upon the organ, the ear would soon weary of this effect and demand a return to the legato. This is not necessarily the case in a piano piece of the kind referred to.

On the other hand, the staccato of the organ is not to be excluded or neglected because of the fact that the nature of the instrument usually calls for legato treatment. The organ staccato is all the more marked in character when judiciously employed, for the very reason that the effect is comparatively exceptional to the usual manner of handling the instrument. Considering this fact, the few thoughts upon this subject which follow may prove of use to the student.

One of the first causes which may prompt the accompanist to the use of the staccato touch, is in case the choir hold back or " drag " the tempo. This is more likely to occur with a large than with a small choir, while, at the same time, it is equally true that the staccato effect upon the organ usually sounds better with a strong rather than with a light registration. This use of the instrument will almost invariably restore the tempo, but may injure the musical effect designed by the composer. It also frequently has a demoralizing influence upon the player himself—in this sense, that an organist who constantly allows himself to resort to this means of steadying a choir, is apt soon to *form a habit* of staccato accompaniment, far beyond the exigencies of the case. He soon gets to think that he can not obtain unity of performance from his singers without it. This is an error, so far as the author's experience goes. The best cure for the fault which demands the continuous staccato accompaniment is rehearsal, after the following manner.

If the organist should perceive that he can not pass a certain point in a given piece without having recourse to the staccato to prevent unsteadiness in tempo, let him immediately rehearse the passage *at the close of the service* in which the " dragging " has occurred. The fault is then fresh in the minds of the singers. Let it be first rehearsed *without* accompaniment, the organist or director beating the time, and beginning at once with the passage in question ; then *with* the organ, taking pains to play the passage as legato as possible, so as *not to help the choir in rhythm or accentuation.* The singers having previously had the purpose of the rehearsal explained, their attention called to the passage, and forced to rely upon themselves as regards promptness, will rarely fall into the same fault again at the same place. Thus future rehearsal is saved. They instinctively remember the special rehearsal when they approach the spot where the fault occurred.

It is well, before closing such rehearsal, to try the piece the third time, beginning at least sixteen measures previous to the critical point. All this need not occupy but a few minutes (*from the moment of commencing*) with an ordinarily intelligent choir. The object of this third trial is that the test may be made *in connection* as well as in the isolated manner first adopted.

It not unfrequently happens that a difficulty, whether of time or intonation, conquered by itself, will cause new trouble when taken in connection with the antecedent portion of the composition. It is but fair that the director should have full assurance that the difficulty has been overcome before closing the rehearsal.

It should be evident, then, that the mere desire to assist singers to a steady performance of a given passage should not, by itself, be accepted as a sufficient justification of a continued use of the staccato touch. The proper guide, as to when and where the staccato should be or may be employed, should be derived from the nature of the phrase itself, *as music.*

To lay down definite rules as to the occasions when this touch may be permitted and when not, would be impossible, owing to the innumerable forms that such phrases may assume. Besides this, the use of the staccato is, to a certain extent, a matter of taste, but should be governed by the nature of the phrase and of the instrument.

Staccato as a means of " steadying the tempo." Abuse of the same.

Rehearsal, instead of undue use of the Staccato.

Final test.

The musical phrase the proper guide for the introduction of this touch.

We have seen that the organ usually calls for a more or less speedy restoration of the legato touch, as giving a sense of repose to the ear.

Taking this into consideration, the student will ordinarily find that *climax passages* will prove best suited to the staccato touch; where the compass gradually rises (in the Soprano more especially), and where notes of longer duration break the continuous staccato effect. This may be illustrated as follows:

EXAMPLE 148.

In the above example, the "slurs" simply show the touch as applied to the instrument. Neither do the staccato marks, as given here, necessarily imply that the notes over which they are placed are to be sung in any especially short and disconnected manner by the voices. The clear articulation of the syllables by the singers will ensure sufficient distinctness.

It will be noticed that we have here, as regards the accompaniment, a contrast between staccato and legato in each alternate measure. This staccato use of the organ may well be considered "legitimate" as lending fire and energy to the passage. In this sense, it is deduced from the nature of the passage as a musical effect, and not from any absolute requirement on the part of the voices. These could render the passage here given without such assistance, but that it *is* an assistance, besides agreeing with the nature of the phrase and aiding the "motion" of the same, is evident.

Prolongation
of the Stac-
cato in short
phrases.

The staccato touch may also be prolonged beyond the limits of one measure, in simple phrases of this kind, especially when the passage leads directly to a climax. Of this we give an illustration in the following example at *a* :

EXAMPLE 149.

It still remains a matter of taste whether the last three chords of the second measure (Example 149, *a*) shall not be played legato. The student should compare the two effects.

At *b*, Example 149, we have a case of the Soprano descending while the male voices rise, admitting of a momentary staccato of three chords. This shows us that the application of this touch need not be confined exclusively to passages in which the melody ascends, although we believe the latter form will more usually be found suited to the staccato ; especially if the passage is to have a strong registration.

Recurring again to Example 148, we note in the third and fourth measures the sustained tone (A) in the Alto, likewise the D in the Tenor. This leads to various comments and the examination of another class of effects. Union of sustained Tones with Staccato.

In the first place, a practical test will show that such a sustained tone does not essentially alter the general staccato effect, when the other notes comprising the various chords are struck in a detached manner. On the contrary—so far as the organ is concerned—the effect is better. The holding tone, being necessarily a common factor of the various harmonies, helps to give the passage a unity which it would otherwise lack, while the staccato chords serve to brighten and diversify it. Thus, the holding tone produces, as it were, a compromise between the legato as the essential nature of the organ and the staccato as opposed to it.

The student will now find that *where such sustained tones can be introduced, the staccato can be prolonged* with good effect, and to a considerably greater extent than where *all the tones* partake of the detached character. Effect of sustained tones upon prolongation of Staccato.

A continued staccato may also be preserved by the organ, without a holding tone, for some time, and without offence to the ear, when the voices thus accompanied themselves assume the role of the holding note ; or at least move in legato style, with notes of longer duration against a staccato accompaniment. The following example, from Spohr's cantata (Op. 98), " God, thou art great," furnishes us with a good illustration : Vocal Legato against Staccato Accompaniment.

EXAMPLE 150.

It is seen that the accompaniment is here continually staccato, but with the second measure the two solo voices, Alto and Bass, enter in legato style. It should be borne in mind that these voices actually represent octaves in pitch, both as compared to each other and the harmonies of the accompaniment, although here written on one staff to economize space. It should also be remembered that the effect we are considering is that of the union of voices and accompaniment *simultaneously heard*, not their separate relation. Compound effect of Example 150.

Limitations in staccato transcriptions for Piano.

We have seen in Chapter IX. that in cases of adaptation of piano accompaniments from the original orchestral score, the figuration of the stringed instruments, together with the fundamental harmonies, is the first thing transcribed. When this has been done, it is frequently impossible to transcribe the wind parts, even if the instrument could sustain them so far as duration of tone is concerned. The impossibility of their transcription arises from the fact of the fingers being fully occupied in executing the figuration above spoken of. Besides this, the wind instruments may be sustaining the identical chord which the stringed instruments give in staccato. The latter can not give way to the former in transcription, on account of preservation of the rhythm.

Advantages of the use of two manuals upon the Organ.

Upon an organ, however, it not unfrequently occurs, in accompaniments of slight technical difficulty, that the wind parts may be executed upon a second manual, thus modifying what would otherwise be too great a prolongation of the pure staccato effect. Our Example 150 is a case in point, and examination of the orchestral score will show the manner in which the composer has avoided a monotony in staccato, while never deviating from the measured rhythm.

We proceed to give a short analysis of Spohr's orchestral treatment of the passage. In this way, we hope to afford the student an idea how a staccato effect may be continuously preserved, and yet so modified as to bring it more into keeping with the nature of the organ.

The staccato chords given in Example 150 represent the identical notes played by the stringed instruments throughout the passage.*

Proportion of Staccato to Legato in Spohr's work. Motive for the same.

The whole composition consists of seventy-two measures, not counting a *postludium* which leads directly to the following and final movement. Within this limit, twelve measures are without accompaniment, and the staccato passages comprise forty-three measures. Should the student ask why Spohr has thus prolonged this effect, the answer may be found in the significance of the initial line of the text:

         "Walk ye, walk, ye hundred thousands!"

The essential march character of the accompaniment is obligatory, or at least highly appropriate. We have already alluded to the modifying influence of the entrance of the solo voices (in the second measure) upon the staccato, qualifying it as by the entrance of wind instruments. This continues until the seventh measure. Here, Spohr introduces the wind instruments themselves as follows:

EXAMPLE 151.

* They differ only by a note or two from Novello's piano score, page 15. When they do so, it is because, in the Novello copy, the transcriber has introduced a few important sustained notes of the wind instruments.

Here, let the student (carefully comparing Example 151 with the corresponding measures of Example 150) notice that the wooden wind instruments (1st Clarionet and 1st Bassoon) enter, as it were, unobserved—that is, they enter *piano* on the unaccented part of the measure. More-over, this tone is "tied" to the first note of the following measure. In this way, they do not obstruct the clear accent and articulation of the two voices on the first beat of measure 8. The instruments assert themselves more decidedly as the crescendo progresses. Influence of the sustained tones upon the Staccato.

At the tenth measure, the 1st Oboe reinforces the 1st Clarionet, this accession being more plainly felt by its entrance on the second beat of the measure as a syncopation. Meantime, the three Trombones complete the remaining harmony parts of this group of instruments.

Thus, with the addition of instruments sustaining tone, and in this sense opposed to the staccato, we have two new "tone-colors" added—namely : the reed instruments and the brass. These latter, especially, contrast strongly in quality of tone, as well as by their legato treatment, with the staccato of the stringed instruments in Example 150. In order that the brass may blend perfectly, without covering either voices or string accompaniment, it will be seen that they enter *piano* when the other instruments and voices have reached the *forte*. (Measure 10.) Contrast in quality of tone between Staccato and Legato.

Notwithstanding these various additions (Example 151), such masterly advantage has been taken of the nature and characteristic tones of these instruments at the particular compass employed, that, if they are well played, the voices will not be covered nor the rhythmic staccato of the stringed instruments concealed. The rhythmic effect remains, while the sharply defined and broken effect of the pure staccato temporarily disappears.

Thus we see on what grounds an expert organist is justified in adding certain holding notes (or chords upon a second manual) which do not exist in a staccato accompaniment as written in the piano score, but which may very well exist in the original orchestral score of the work. On the other hand, if the work be originally written for piano, he may add such holding tones for the organ, on the ground that it *would be done* were the work to be scored for orchestra. Addition of sustained tones justified by this example.

Although the use of two manuals will frequently give the truest transcription in cases of this kind, especially if *contrasting* qualities of tone are desired, one manual will often prove adequate for the purpose. Thus, our present example might be treated as follows upon the Swell Organ : Staccato with sustained tones upon one Manual.

EXAMPLE 152.

The general legato is here resumed at the tenth measure, on account of the momentary prominence that the wind instruments gain at this point. (See Example 151.) Another reason for resuming the legato here, and one which undoubtedly governed Spohr, in his orchestral setting, is the cadence of the modulation to G minor. The ear should not be allowed to doubt for a moment as to whither this is tending. The staccato, although not precisely insufficient for

With two Manuals. the purpose, does not accomplish this in so complete a manner as the sustained form with connected harmonies. With two manuals, the treatment might be as follows:

EXAMPLE 153

The pedal assumes the legato in the tenth measure for the same reason given under Example 152.

It is evidently advantageous to have some idea of the nature of the parts usually played by the wind instruments in orchestral scores. This knowledge will enable the organist to modify such continuous staccato passages as may present themselves, with more or less certainty of not violating the composer's intentions. It is not necessary that holding notes thus introduced by him should be the identical sustained tones of the orchestral score; but if so, all the better. It may very likely be the case that the organist is not familiar with the orchestral score, or can not get access to the same, or, again, that the reading of such a score would be a "sealed book" to him. It suffices for the purpose that the tones sustained do not assert themselves too radically. To this end, it is usually best to keep them in the middle of the harmony, and sometimes even lower. Besides this, in case two manuals are employed, the second manual should be so registered as to be subordinate to the first in quantity of tone.

Choice of tones to be sustained against a Staccato Accompaniment.

If we did not know what this specific case requires, the following treatment, on the principle above advanced, would be appropriate as an organ effect for one manual qualifying the staccato:

EXAMPLE 154.

Other sustained tones may also be employed, as for instance :

EXAMPLE 155.

In selecting the form to be employed thus, the relation of the sustained tone to the vocal part should always be considered. The student will perceive that the *principle* here involved is essentially identical with that which we have already considered under the head of "Adaptation of Piano and Orchestral Accompaniments to the Organ." (See Chapter IX., pages 100, 101.)

Relation of sustained tone to vocal part.

When the staccato accompaniment is sufficiently varied melodically *in the upper tones* of the chords which constitute it, these upper tones may sometimes be treated as a legato melody, when relief from continued staccato is desired. Our former illustration, treated thus, would assume the following form :

Upper tone of Staccato changed to Legato.

EXAMPLE 156.

In this case, such legato treatment would, of course, give the opening measures quite a different significance from that intended by the composer. It is, nevertheless, identical with the means he has subsequently employed. (See Measure 8, Example 151.) With the latter half of the fifth measure (see Example 150), it would already cease its independent melodic progress, and ally itself to the voices in unison.

This form is here applied to this example only as a specimen of treatment which may sometimes be found useful in *other* continued staccato passages.

Where florid bass passages occur, accompanied by full chords, it is frequently preferable to play these chords with the staccato touch. This holds good, whether the bass passages are intended to be executed by the pedals or mannals. The strictest legato should meantime be maintained in the bass passages themselves—the same constituting the *essential figure* which it is desired should predominate and characterize the piece. The staccato renders the accompaniment transparent, and the ear is the more readily attracted to the figuration in question. An illustration of this treatment may be found in the following quotation from the chorus, "Fixed in his everlasting seat," from Handel's oratorio of "Samson:"

"Florid" Bass passages with Staccato chords.

EXAMPLE 157.

The manual here supports the pedal in the octave. The mode of avoiding interference of both hands upon the same note should here be noticed, and the student should compare the above with the passage as given in the piano score of the oratorio.

Avoidance of "string-tone" in soft Staccato Registration. It has been remarked that staccato passages generally prove most effective upon the organ with at least a *mezzo-forte* combination. This is because stops of slower speech are assisted to the short, prompt utterance required, by means of stops of quicker speech combined with them.

When it is desired to make use of a soft staccato effect, the combination requires more care. In such case, string-toned stops should usually be avoided, certainly never used in this manner alone. As we have elsewhere seen, these stops are only properly suited to legato-playing, if their best characteristics are to be made evident.

Of other applications of the staccato touch, the following may be briefly alluded to:

Melody with *ad libitum* Staccato Accompaniment. When a melody which has previously moved principally in quarter notes suddenly changes to half-note motion, accompanied by legato chords, the organist may find it advisable to change the accompaniment to the staccato. We give an example of such a melody in the Bass. On account of the relatively low pitch of the voices, the staccato accompaniment serves here the double purpose of continuing the rhythm, and calling attention to the melody itself.

EXAMPLE 158.

An example analogous to the above, but presenting some differences, is furnished by the ending of Barnby's anthem, " O risen Lord !"

EXAMPLE 159.

This example agrees with the former in that the piece has been characterized throughout by quarter-note motion, and suddenly changes to notes of longer duration as it nears its close. The staccato of the accompaniment, however, now serves the purpose of a *stretto* or climax, preserving the sense of motion to the close. In this it aids (and also contrasts with) the Tenor vocal part, which maintains a series of syncopations. The rhythmic accentuation is hereby perfectly preserved in the voices without the aid of the accompaniment. Still, the climax is much heightened by the powerful and independent accents of the accompaniment, the effect being equivalent to a union of two separate rhythms.

We may now leave the student to judge for himself as to when and in what manner he may avail himself of the staccato touch upon the organ. If he has thoroughly digested the ideas advanced in the previous pages, he should find no trouble in deciding in what cases the pure staccato touch should be used, and when it is better to employ it with accompanying holding tones or chords. In either case, he should use it sparingly.

Preservation of rhythm with syncopation.

CHAPTER XIV.

THOROUGH-BASS, AND PLAYING FROM VOCAL SCORE.

Supposed
benefit of the
study.
THE impression seems to prevail largely among a certain class of organ students (to wit, such as have had but little theoretical instruction), that the study of Thorough-Bass will, in some mysterious way, greatly assist them in playing the organ.

The manner in which Thorough-Bass has been taught, in certain manuals and by many teachers in this country, has been little less than a thorough humbug and waste of time and money. This so far as the acquisition or application of the " art of playing church-music from figures"— as they please to call it—is concerned.

The object of this chapter is simply to explain the ancient and modern value of a figured bass, and give the pupil, if may be, a clear conception of its former use and application in accompaniment. A technical treatise on this subject would be out of place here ; besides which, we have assumed (see close of Preliminary Remarks) that the pupil making use of this work is already familiar with the fundamental principles of harmony.

Relation be-
tween Thor-
ough-Bass
and Harmony.
And first to get a clear idea of the difference between Thorough-Bass and Harmony.

Harmony is an extremely elastic word, frequently used in a loose way in speaking of treatment involving a knowledge of the advanced laws of musical theory, while, at the same time, it includes and covers the subject of Thorough-Bass. This latter, strictly considered, is nothing but a series of figures placed over (or under) a given Bass. By means of these figures, the player recognizes the remaining notes which he is to play in conjunction with each bass note given : each bass note forming one of the component intervals of the several chords thus resulting. It is evident that the thorough-bass figures simply call attention to *each chord considered by itself*, and without reference to the proper connection of a given chord with that which precedes or succeeds it. To accomplish such connection, and give us a proper succession of chords, whose constituent parts shall have a good, natural progression under established rules, is the specific mission of Harmony. With this, Thorough-Bass has, as a system, nothing whatever to do.

Evils attend-
ing the use of
the figures
without more
extended har-
monic know-
ledge.
When a pupil who simply knew the meaning of the figures attempted to play a common church tune, the result was a crude performance, with three parts constantly given to the right hand and the bass only to the left. This not only led to a mere mechanical performance, but to a total disregard of the proper flow of parts and interconnection of the chords among themselves ; besides being subversive of the proper mode of handling the organ as an instrument.

The absurdity of introducing a figured bass into our older church-music books, is made further manifest by the misplacement of the vocal parts to which it gave rise. In the first place, the *natural order* of parts—namely : Soprano, Alto, Tenor, and Bass—was destroyed by placing the Soprano immediately above the Bass. This was done in order that the Soprano, as the highest part, might determine the particular form of the chord desired. Melody and Bass thus being given, a person at all conversant with the subject could very nearly guess at the remaining tones necessary to complete the harmony. The simple structure of most of these tunes required no figuration whatever, the score being given at the same time. Still the Bass was figured more or less carefully. Meantime the Tenor was written on the first or upper staff of the score, the Alto upon the second *above* the Soprano. This unnatural mode of placing the voices made it materially more difficult for the beginner to learn to "read from score"—that is, to take in the chord with one glance of the eye, allotting to each voice its proper part. The true construction of a vocal score demands that the natural order of voices, as to pitch, be followed. In this way, what the ear hears corresponds logically with that which the eye perceives. But the American hymn-tune willed it otherwise and disturbed this symmetry. *(margin: Disarrangement of "natural order" in the Score.)*

Even with the natural order of the score changed as above described, it was an easier task to acquire the facility of reading the several parts, than to learn the whole system of thorough-bass figuring ; at least with such expertness as to be able to apply it instantly. Besides this, playing from score brought with it the immeasurable advantage of directing the player's attention to the *melodic progress* of the several parts. This the figuring did not do, but concentrated the student's attention upon each chord as an individual item. Thus, consecutive octaves and fifths, undesirable "doublings" of certain intervals, and the like, were frequently made. The church-books, of later years, have indeed dropped the useless figuring, but neither the Tenor nor Alto has yet been restored to its proper place in the score in books of the class referred to. *(margin: Advantage of "Playing from Score" rather than from Figures.)*

In such books as have been printed with a separate accompaniment, this has been done. These remarks do not, of course, apply to the modern "Hymnals," "Hymnaries," and the like, where, for economy of space, the tune is printed upon two staves in so-called "compressed" or "short" score. This form gives the accompanist a literal transcription of the voices at their proper relation to each other. The only possible objection to this mode of setting the tunes, is the fact that it compels the Tenor voices to sing from the bass clef. This rarely proves any real objection, owing to the simplicity of the music usually treated thus. *(margin: "Compressed" or "short" Score.)*

The use of a figured bass in our church-music is a thing of the past—a custom virtually extinct—if, indeed, it ever amounted to a custom in this country. It had a *learned look*, but a practical use we firmly believe it never had in any broad sense.

What, then, is the present value of the study of Thorough-Bass, and whence came its former reputation ?

The value of the study is as great to-day as it ever was, for it gives the student a knowledge of all possible chord-formations, and classifies them for his convenience. In one point of view, this study is more important than ever, as the tendency of modern times has been to develop "new harmonies," so called. In truth, there is no such thing possible, nor have any "new chords," strictly speaking, been constructed since the day of Bach and Handel, and even before their time. There has been, however, a modern application of old principles, resulting in some forms rarely used by the old masters. A good knowledge of Thorough Bass will easily enable the student to discover the laws which govern these apparently strange formations, and reduce them easily to first principles. *(margin: Present value of the study.)*

Use of Thorough-Bass in former times.

When we turn to the *practical* application of Thorough-Bass as made use of in former times, we soon recognize the reason of the high value set upon it, and upon the abilities of those competent to make a ready and expert use of it.

In the days when this system was established,[*] engraved or printed music was scarce and expensive. Especially in the old churches and cathedrals of Europe, manuscript music was the rule, and printed copies the rare exception. As separate parts had to be furnished to the singers, it was a great saving of labor to be able to hand the organist a simple bass part figured. Otherwise it would have been necessary to write out all the four parts and condense them for the organ, not to speak of full chords sometimes required. The saving of labor in case of a whole mass or long cantata is evident.

Thus, for composer, organist, and copyist, a figured bass was a labor-saving invention—a species of musical " short-hand."

A competent knowledge of Harmony preceding the use of a figured Bass.

The knowledge required by this mode of writing had a far greater significance than the mere deciphering of the chord by means of figures. It involved a familiarity with the whole harmonic system and the laws governing the *progression of chords among themselves.* To commit the multiplication-table to memory is not to become thereby a mathematician; but the mathematician uses the multiplication-table as a familiar and necessary acquirement. So the expert *harmonist*, of the times referred to, turned back (in a scientific sense) to the figured bass as to an elementary formula which showed him the various chords required. It was expected of him to give the correct harmonic *progressions* of the composition, as well as merely play chord for chord as denoted by the respective figures. This implied a harmonic knowledge far exceeding the mere mechanical interpretation of the thorough-bass figuration itself.

Accompaniment not necessarily coincident with vocal melody.

In accompanying in this manner (from a bass part only) it might easily happen that the player would not give the same form of the chord *melodically* as was represented by the voices. This was a matter of trifling importance, so long as the voices were supported by the same chord *harmonically.* The student is doubtless familiar with the rule that where no figure is annexed to a given note, the common chord of which that note forms the fundamental bass is indicated. From this circumstance arose the custom, in the old figuration, of giving the accompanist a hint as to the particular form desired by placing the figures 8, 5, or 3 over a given bass note, in cases other than where a " resolution " was to be expressed. Where the melody as well as the bass was given, as in case of our older American church-music books referred to, such figuration was manifestly useless.

" Basso Continuo."

As the vocal bass might cease at times, the instrumental bass, or fundamental part given the organist, was called " *Basso Continuo*," or simply *Continuo*. It was the player's only guide. As a simple illustration of this, Luther's chorale, " *Ein' feste Burg* " would be indicated thus:

EXAMPLE 160.

In this manner, the identical melody might often be followed. The more important use of the figured bass was, naturally, in compositions of much larger scope, and where the particular inversion of the chord was of secondary importance to a correct harmonic progression. This was particularly the case when the orchestra was employed with the organ.

The student may now perceive that Thorough Bass played a great *rôle* in the early days of accompaniment. All the cantatas and oratorios of Bach and Handel, in which the organ was calculated upon as an important element in the accompaniment, were originally composed with only a " continuo " to represent the duty of the organist. This is greatly to be regretted, for the weakness of the system (with all its convenience) lies in the fact that such a bass may be variously interpreted as to inversions, etc., especially when not fully figured. This is frequently the case with the old masters. An explanation of this may doubtless be found in our knowledge that many of these compositions were written in haste ; and furthermore that Bach usually, and Handel frequently, played the organ themselves at the performance of their compositions. They would, of course, require the least possible memoranda of the treatment proposed.

The Organ part in the Oratorios, etc., of Bach and Handel.

Even in the chamber music of that day, the harpsichord-player—the forerunner of our modern pianist—was expected to accompany concerted music for voices or instruments from a figured bass.

Use of Figures in Chamber Music.

The following example, from Corelli's sonatas for two Violins, Violoncello, and Harpsichord illustrates this :

EXAMPLE 161.

* " Arcangelo Corelli, founder of the Roman school (or what may now be termed the ancient school) of violinists. Born at Fusignano, Italy, in 1653. Published his first twelve sonatas at Rome about 1683." For particulars regarding Corelli, his life and works, see Moore's " Encyclopedia of Music," page 225.

A defect of the figured-bass system shows itself here in the second measure where the figuring $\frac{5}{4}\,\frac{7}{}$ occurs. It is manifest that in cases of this kind the actual duration of the dissonance suspended can not be given. In fact, the inference is that the resolution of the dissonance occurs

simultaneously with the progression of the bass, thus :

The same indefiniteness naturally exists in other forms where the chord or its inversions change upon a given bass note, as in the figuring 5–6 : 7–6 : 9–8, etc. The accompanist helped himself here in two ways : first, by a glance at the full score, if he had it before him ; secondly, by his ear, and his sense, as a musician, of the requirements of the phrase. This was an easier matter than might be supposed ; as in the old masters, of what might be called the " figured-bass period," there was a certain mannerism in the treatment of cadences with which the accompanist might be supposed to be familiar.

When rapid passages occurred, in the stringed or other accompanying instruments of a concerted movement, the harmonic support which the accompanist was to give upon the piano or organ usually became simpler.*

We give as an illustration a few measures of the opening *allegro* from the same sonata :

EXAMPLE 162.

---

* Upon the principle that where harmonies are intricate, with much modulation, etc., the ear requires time to appreciate their purpose and effect. The judicious composer writes the movement accordingly in a moderately slow time at least. For a similar reason, quick tempos, with florid figuration, demand a comparatively simple harmonic basis ; the " passages " themselves being usually diatonic in character, or, when chromatic, being based upon very simple harmonies.

Here the simple chords are given upon which the violin passages (abounding in single and double passing notes) are founded. This would not sound wholly satisfactory to the modern ear if played upon a grand piano of to-day. There would be too great an interference between these passing notes and the resonance of the piano. It must be remembered, however, that the old harpsichords and early pianos did not possess such resonance. For the above reason, we do not find such harmonic freedom allowed when the accompaniment was intended for the organ. Simple as the given bass in Example 162 appears, if the student would make evident to himself the harmonic expertness required to properly accompany the passage, let him attempt to harmonize the first three measures in four parts, without falling into the error of consecutive octaves or fifths. Practically, a freedom was allowed in this respect, by allowing one part to disappear temporarily, and letting the chords consist sometimes of three and sometimes of four or more tones. *(Character of the instrument as affecting the figured Accompaniment.)*

One application of Thorough-Bass, which lingered even after its general use had been superseded by carefully written accompaniments, was its employment to indicate the harmonies to vocal recitatives. These the accompanist played upon the harpsichord, or upon the organ if the performance was held where an organ could be made available. The orchestra meanwhile waited until the next "concerted" accompaniment. *(Thorough-Bass as Accompaniment to Recitatives.)*

Almost all the recitatives of Bach, Handel, and Haydn were written to a mere figured-bass part. It found use in the opera as well; and even in such a work as Mozart's "Don Juan," we find the recitatives figured in many cases. This was usually the case in the Italian operas, until a comparatively recent date. The older masters occasionally wrote separate accompaniments in the original score to their recitatives. In such case, these were specifically called "*accompanied*" *recitatives*. Illustrations of these in Handel's "Messiah" are, among others, the "Comfort ye my people," and "And lo! the angel of the Lord came upon them."

After a long time, the interpolation of the harpsichord or piano tone in works of this kind began to be felt as incongruous, when the other numbers were provided with full orchestral accompaniment. The same objection could not apply to the organ, owing to its capacity for sustaining tone. The result was the assignment of the chords which the figured bass represented to the stringed instruments of the orchestra. All modern piano editions of these works are now given with the accompaniment to the recitatives and other passages fully written out. Nothing is left to the option of the accompanist as to the form of the chords themselves. *(Incongruous effect of the Piano or Harpsichord interrupting the Orchestra.)*

Playing from vocal score, not to speak of orchestral, is a much more valuable accomplishment than the mere expert deciphering of a figured bass. To acquire it, the students should first be familiar with all harmonic progressions, resolutions of chords, etc. He should then commence with simple four-part pieces in which the middle voices have little or no independent motion. His harmonic knowledge will speedily enable him to recognize at a glance the given chord, its particular form, inversion, etc., although printed upon four staves. The same knowledge will also enable him to *anticipate* the succeeding chord or progression in many cases. *(Playing from Vocal Score—its relative value. How to acquire it.)*

In doing this, the eye may either glance downward (from the Soprano), through the score, or upward, from the Bass. The latter method will probably be found preferable in the majority of cases. It will be governed, however, by the motion of a given part; as, for instance, if the Soprano moves while the Bass does not, and *vice versa*.

When the student has acquired a tolerable degree of facility in playing pieces of a simple harmonic character, he may proceed to such as contain more motion in the middle parts, and finally to those where all the voices have an independent, melodic progression.

Mendelssohn's four-part songs furnish good material for such practice.

In regard to the requirements demanded in playing from orchestral score, the student will find a suggestive and valuable, although by no means exhaustive, article under the head of "Playing from Score," in Moore's "Encyclopedia of Music."

In conclusion and likewise in recapitulation, the student will perceive that the use of Thorough-Bass, as a means of playing accompaniments, is practically a thing of the past, but that its value in theoretical study has not diminished, and can not do so in the slightest degree.

He who qualifies himself to be a *thoroughly good* harmonist will find no great difficulty in playing from a figured bass, should such occasion present itself. Of course, the accompanists of former days acquired, from constantly using this system, a readiness in playing from it, especially at sight and in a comparatively quick tempo, which would not readily be found now. The broadcast dissemination of musical literature, at comparatively low prices, in which the accompaniments are fully written out, has done away with the necessity of such an application of Thorough-Bass in our day.

Such organists as have occasion to use much manuscript music in their choirs, may, however, find it a convenient mode of short-hand writing, as saving the labor of writing out their own part in full.

CHAPTER XV.

ACCOMPANIMENT WITH ORCHESTRA.

But few, perhaps, of those making use of this book will have the opportunity offered them of playing the organ part in works composed for voices, full orchestral accompaniment and organ. Nevertheless, there must come a "first time" when some young organist of ability will be called upon to make this experience.

For such an one—and what talented and faithful student may not, at least, aspire to it?—it is hoped this chapter may contain useful hints; while, in an artistic point of view, the subject can not fail to have some interest even to those to whom the practical experience may never come.

Before proceeding to examine the conditions governing this class of accompaniment, we will quote, and comment upon, certain passages bearing upon this subject from Berlioz's "Art of Instrumentation." Hector Berlioz on this subject.

Under the head of "The Organ," he says :

*" It is doubtless possible to blend the organ with the divers constituent elements of the orchestra ; and it has even been many times done, but it is strangely derogatory to this majestic instrument to reduce it to this secondary condition " (namely, of subordinate accompaniment).
. . . . . " Moreover, it should be felt that its smooth, equal, and uniform sonorousness never entirely melts into the variously characterized sounds of the orchestra, and that there seems to exist between these two musical powers a secret antipathy." . . . .

" Whenever I have heard the organ played at the same time with the orchestra, it has seemed to me to produce a destestable effect, and to impair that of the orchestra instead of augmenting it."

No matter what rank different individuals may assign to Berlioz as a composer, there are, at least, no two opinions as to his intimate acquaintance with special orchestral effects.

As to his stricture upon the use of the organ with orchestra being "derogatory to the majestic instrument," our greatest masters in oratorio, Bach, Handel, and Mendelssohn, have evidently not thought so. They have, on the contrary, relied upon the organ in all of their works of this kind, for some of their grandest effects. In the most modern treatment of the modern orchestra, we find composers still resorting to it, as a means of effect unattainable in any other way. Of this, we have an ultra illustration in the " *Christus*" of Liszt, and (in purely instrumental work) in the same composer's symphonic poem, entitled " *Die Hunnenschlacht.*" Use of the Organ with Orchestra by recognised masters.

---

* Berlioz's " Art of Instrumentation. "   Novello's edition, page 127.

"Uniform
Sonorous-
ness." "Anti-
pathy between
Organ and
Orchestra,"
etc.

As to its " uniform sonorousness " proving an objection, the simple fact is that it need not, and should not be employed at such uniform sonorousness. On the contrary, the tone should be varied, through the skill of the performer, to suit the requirements of the composition. Most organs now found in concert-halls, here as well as in Europe, are provided with mechanical means to assist the performer in such cases.

As to the " secret antipathy which seems to exist between these two musical powers," there is a certain amount of truth in Berlioz's remarks ; but this " antipathy " is not radical, but qualified by various conditions which we will consider later.

From the third quotation, we can only deduce the opinion, that Berlioz was unfortunate enough never to have heard the organ properly played in connection with the orchestra ; for the effect, in such case, is generally considered, both by professional critics and amateurs, to be any thing but " detestable." Indeed, those who have had the opportunity of hearing a *good* performance with orchestra *and* organ of such choruses (and many more might be cited) as Handel's " Hallelujah !" from the " Messiah ;" Bach's " Ye thunders, ye lightnings," from the " Passion Music according to St. Matthew ;" or the " Thanks be to God," from Mendelssohn's " Elijah," can scarcely be satisfied with ever so good a performance by the largest chorus and orchestra, *without* the organ.

We dwell upon this point that the student may not be rendered doubtful in his own opinion, should he meet with a hostile one from so eminent an authority, in matters pertaining to combined tone effects, as Berlioz.

Having seen that the practice of the masters has been to make extensive use of the organ in connection with the orchestra, let us now examine the grounds which Berlioz had for making the criticisms given. Although exaggerated, they do not proceed from mere idle prejudice, and are therefore worthy of examination. In this way, we shall ascertain in what the " secret antipathy " referred to consists, and the student will gain a clearer idea of *what he should avoid*, before proceeding to consider *what he should do*.

When voices sing or an orchestra plays " in tune," conventionally speaking, they sing or play in *perfect* tune as compared with our keyed instruments, the piano, and, more especially, the organ. These two are *never* in perfect tune, mathematically speaking. The modern system of tuning distributes the inequalities of the scale among different intervals of that scale, and in such a way that perfect octaves are obtained, but the other intervals slightly modified. The ear accepts them, however, as practically " in tune." This system is called " The Equal Temperament."*

Besides this, a large organ is never *strictly* in tune, even upon the compromise of equal temperament ; not even when the tuners have but just left the instrument. This is owing to the greatly varying size, material, and relative exposure of the different pipes to atmospheric changes. This applies likewise to barometric as well as thermometric influences.

We have also seen (in Chapter I.) that the principles upon which the Mixtures of the organ are constructed, introduce into any given harmony a series of tones wholly foreign to that harmony. This is utterly opposed to the nature of the orchestra, and, if allowed to assert itself in connection with it, the effect might well be pronounced " detestable."

This is by no means saying that the Mixtures may *never* be employed in connection with the orchestra, but simply that they are only to be used when the great force of combined orchestral and choral effects, upon a large scale, conceals their *harmonic* character. This is,

---

* It is necessarily impossible to treat, with even measurable fulness, of this important subject here. Such students as may not be familiar with it are referred to an able exposition of the same in Cornell's " Primer of Modern Tonality," Chapter VI., page 33. G. Schirmer, New York.

indeed, the same principle upon which they are to be used in simple organ accompaniment. In this case, however, still greater care is to be exercised that their individual character is *wholly* absorbed in the general harmonic mass.

In order, then, that the best effects may be obtained from the organ in the connection of which we are now speaking, it is necessary for the organist to forego all attempts at display. He must so handle his instrument that the listener experiences the effect of a great pervading force, sustaining the whole harmonic superstructure without obtruding its individual tone upon the ear. *The Organist should here sink the individuality of his instrument.*

It is certainly the part of an artist to sink his own individuality and that of his instrument in the more perfect rendering of a master work requiring the combined resources of organ and orchestra. Where the effect thus produced is more sublime than without it, it can scarcely be deemed "derogatory to the majestic instrument" to be called upon to lend a subordinate assistance to a more perfect and therefore more artistic result.

The two qualities of tone which the organist must be cautious of employing are the Mixtures and the Manual Reeds.

We need say no more as regards the Mixtures.

The reeds do not assimilate well with the orchestral tone, except in passages where they lend increased power to the general *fortissimo* without their characteristic quality being perceived. In this respect, their use is nearly identical with that of the Mixtures, although, if in good tune, they may be introduced somewhat earlier. Should they be employed in soft passages, they would (as imitative stops) compare unfavorably in tone and intonation with the actual orchestral instruments from which their names are derived. They may sometimes be employed (as well as the Flutes) in performances upon a comparatively small scale ; as, for instance, when the orchestra is represented virtually by the stringed instruments only. In such case, the organ may supply the actual wind parts with an effect more or less closely approximating the composer's intention in the original orchestral score. *Reed-stops with Orchestra.*

The chief value of the organ, as an addition to an orchestral accompaniment, is unquestionably the gain resulting from the deep foundation furnished by pedal tones. Nothing in the orchestra equals these in gravity, weight, nor in ability to sustain the same. Here, the effect of the "uniform sonorousness" frequently produces results of little less than electrical effect. *Value of the Pedal tones with Orchestra.*

The lowest tone of the orchestra is the low E $\begin{array}{c}\text{♮}\end{array}$ of the Double Bass (Contrabasso), sounding an octave lower than written. The pedal organ, with sixteen-foot stops drawn, gives us a major third lower yet—namely : $\begin{array}{c}\text{♮}\end{array}$ and, should the instrument be provided with a pedal-stop of 32 feet, we obtain tones *two octaves* and a major third lower than the written notes, and one octave and a major third lower than any sounds producible by orchestral instruments. It is not the mere additional compass which alone makes these tones valuable, but their power of indefinitely sustaining them, and their pervading quality.

Almost valueless as musical sounds, considered by themselves, they become of infinite importance when serving as a foundation to a grand and massive superstructure.

The manual-stops best uniting themselves with the orchestral tone are the Diapasons and Flutes (eight, four, and even two feet), especially in *piano* and *mezzo-forte* accompaniments. The sixteen-foot stops of the manuals should not be employed where the accompaniment is held *piano*, as the lower octaves which they give would cause the same to be heard in an unpleasant way, when the orchestral standard is essentially eight feet. This is especially the case in *Stops most readily blending with Orchestra. Use of Sixteen-foot Manual Tone.*

fugued movements where the theme is led off in the Soprano, Alto, or Tenor, and where the organ has no sustaining *harmonies*, but simply supports the voices in unison. In this latter instance, it is well to avoid the sixteen-foot tone even in fortissimo. An illustration of this avoidance of sixteen-foot tone would be the *commencement* of the following chorus from Handel's " Samson :"

EXAMPLE 163.

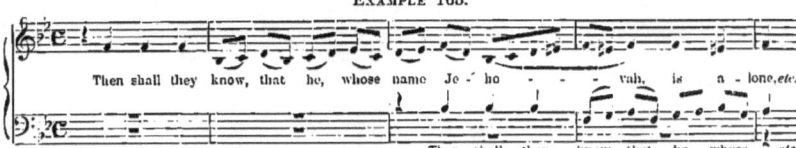

Then shall they know, that he, whose name Je - ho - - - vah, is a - lone, *etc.*

Then shall they know, that he whose, *etc.*

After the entrance of the Bass, the sixteen-foot stops may appropriately be added. Novello advises the opening of this chorus with Full Organ without reeds. Such registration would more plainly call attention to the underlying octaves than would the Full Organ complete. For another example of this kind, see the opening of the chorus, " And the glory of the Lord shall be revealed," from Handel's " Messiah."

If the fugue theme leads in the Bass, there can rarely be any objection to the use of " Doubles."

Deduction from preceding remarks. The deduction from the preceding remarks is evidently this, that it is the duty of the organist (1) so to subdue his instrument that it blend into the general effect without being specially perceived as to its own tone-color—in a word, that it is to be *felt* rather than heard : (2) except in *fortissimo* passages, its Diapasons and Flutes are principally of value, not excluding the use of even the Full Organ when the size and power of orchestra and chorus admit the same. Even in such case, the subordinate relation is to be preserved. Let us now proceed further, and consider *what* the organist should play and what he should omit.

The vocal parts as a guide. By general consent of the best authorities, his primary duty is to support the voices by playing the vocal parts, *not as condensed in a piano accompaniment*, but reading from the vocal score. In addition to this, to support the instrumental bass wherever requisite, when the vocal bass may for the time be silent. This would ordinarily give the organist but four strict parts to play. But it so happens that, as a " filling-in " effect, chords of eight and even ten tones are sometimes desirable. Thus, in the chorus (No. 35) from " Elijah," Mendelssohn has given the organ accompaniment as follows at *a :*

EXAMPLE 164.

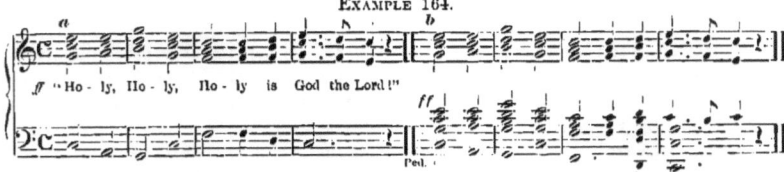

ff " Ho - ly, Ho - ly, Ho - ly is God the Lord!"

Fuller Harmonies. If the student will turn to this chorus, and notice the effect produced by the burst of all the voices, full orchestra and organ, as a response to the Soprano solo ("Holy, Holy," etc.) which precedes it *without accompaniment*, he will see the justice of the treatment at *b*, Example 164.

The form as given by Mendelssohn (at *a*) is evidently intended as a sketch to guide the player. This is shown by the great distance between the bass and the chords of the right hand ;

as well as in the third measure by the extremely inferior effect of the upper F, as compared with the lower, given to the pedal bass.

It may also occur when voices syllabically repeat a number of tones belonging to the same chord, that the effect may be enhanced by simply sustaining such chord upon the organ. This too, not unfrequently, without reference to passing tones. From this we see that even the vocal parts can only be a guide, not a final decision, as to the organist's duty.

Unfortunately, Bach and Handel have written out no organ-parts to their great works, as they played them or would have them played. They have left us only a figured bass, which, as we have seen in the previous chapter, may be variously interpreted as to inversions, etc. Neither have they indicated when and where the organ should cease, the figured bass frequently continuing (for the benefit of the harpsichord-player of that day) when the use of the organ is objectionable on technical as well as æsthetic grounds. Bach and Handel.

As, then, neither Bach nor Handel has furnished us with any specific examples, but merely with general indications of their purpose, we therefore turn to Mendelssohn, who, as the connecting link between the ancient and modern schools, thoroughly understood the capabilities of the organ in this direction ; and has also furnished the best specimens of oratorio since the time of the two musical giants before mentioned.

In two instances, at least, Mendelssohn has shown his desire to have the organ handled *in a particular way* in connection with the orchestra. These instances are his "*Lobgesang*" (Hymn of Praise, Op. 52) and his "Elijah," Op. 70. Mendelssohn.

To show the importance he placed upon the effect of the organ in these compositions, it suffices to call attention to the fact that, in the first mentioned work, he has carefully written out the accompaniment as he desires it played, even to hints in registration.

In the latter work, the orchestral score contains only indications of *when* the organ is to be used, and *when not*, by means of the terms "*Senza Organo*" (without organ), and "*Col Organo*" (with organ), placed under the contra-bass part. Mendelssohn subsequently wrote out an organ-part to "Elijah," evidently for the purpose of assuring the proper treatment of the instrument, without trusting to the taste and judgment of the performer. This organ-part is now published separately (by Simrock, in Bonn), in sheet-music form, and bears upon its title the remark—"from the original manuscript of the composer." This accompaniment is not so carefully prepared as that to the "Hymn of Praise"—that is, Mendelssohn has written it out without continuously indicating the proper use of the pedals, as to their employment in the upper or lower octave. He has also sometimes omitted the evidently desirable "filling-in" of full chords, as in Example 164. He has so constructed the part (probably as a matter of personal convenience in writing) as though it were intended for a so-called cabinet or reed organ. It is, of course, easy for an experienced organist to supply what is lacking in this respect. Manner of indicating use and cessation of the Organ in full scores.

Turning to the "Hymn of Praise," we proceed to give certain illustrations and to analyze to some extent the treatment. By a careful study of these and the following examples, the student should not only be enabled to gain an insight into Mendelssohn's purpose, but also be able to deduce therefrom valuable information as to the proper treatment of the organ in similar works,* which chance to be unprovided with a special accompaniment by the composer. Mendelssohn's "Hymn of Praise."

In the first chorus of the "Hymn of Praise," the voices, with orchestra and organ, present themselves as follows :

---

* Mendelssohn also wrote out an organ part to Handel's "Israel in Egypt," for use in England, and published by the Handel Society of London in their folio edition of Handel's works.

EXAMPLE 165.

In this example, the first thing which attracts our notice is that the progression of the voices is not followed by the organ in the first two measures. Even the voices themselves do not give the *essential* rhythm of the piece, which is represented by the figure of the Second Violins. Violas, and Basses, thus: It will be seen that the Horns and Trombones likewise assist this figure in the latter half of each of these two measures. Meantime the organ sustains the chords, *rising with the accent of each measure* in unison with the soprano voices.

EXAMPLE 105.

This, in the first two measures, brings the Soprano voices lower than the organ accompaniment on the second (unaccented) half of these measures, even as compared with the eight-foot registration only. This is partly compensated for by the progression of the 1st Trumpet, in unison with the Sopranos. The student should endeavor to make evident to his mental ear the bright tone of this latter instrument. The whole instrumentation is evidently based upon the assumption of a large chorus. This shows us that where the harmony changes but slightly (of the five measures given four are represented by the chord of B flat), it is unessential for the organ to repeat the rhythm of either voices or instruments. The essential *motion* is kept intact by the orchestra.

The mission of the Organ to blend together the tone-mass.

It is then evident that the mission of the organ, in such cases, is to reduce the passage to its essential *harmonies*. In so doing, it exerts a strong influence as a "blending-in" effect and means of unity. The student should bear in mind that, as the accompaniment is here marked *ff*, other octaves are sounding in the organ part, besides those which appear to the eye.

It may be said here that as a full exposition of this subject would greatly exceed our space (through the necessity of giving many examples in score), it is expected that the student will, at least, supply himself with the piano scores of the works referred to for purposes of comparison.

For this reason, comparatively familiar and easily accessible works have been selected from which to draw our illustrations. This being assumed, we return to our former example.

The Organ considered as a member of the orchestral body.

The organ proceeds, in the general manner shown, for fifteen measures, and on reaching the "*Animato*" (sixteenth measure from the vocal opening) ceases. Subsequently, it resumes, during the last seven measures of the *Animato*, to cease again at the "*Allegro di molto*" ("Praise the Lord with lute and harp").

This calls attention to the fact that the organ is not here being used as a *continuously* accompanying instrument, but as essentially one of the orchestral family, mingling its tone at stated intervals in the harmonic mass for a given purpose. The cessation, as well as the re-entrance, of its tone, is one of any composer's most decided means of heightening the effect, and of this Mendelssohn always avails himself.

EXAMPLE 166.

Example of Sixteen-foot Manual Registration.

We have, in the above example, an illustration of the manner in which the organ may be employed when but one vocal part for the time being continues the piece. The stringed instruments here supply the rhythmic accompaniment continuously (for which see piano score), while the Oboes and Horns reinforce the voices in unison and in the octave.

The student should carefully note the effect of the sixteen-foot registration. Were the passage given to the bass voices, the accompaniment would "overlie" the voices. This, with the sixteen-foot registration, would be too thick and gloomy, especially in case of a small chorus. As it is, the sixteen-foot stop "underlies" the Altos, and does not disturb the clearness of the passing notes given them.

EXAMPLE 167.

EXAMPLE 167.

We call attention to the "pedal point" in the accompaniment to Example 167, as occupying three out of the four measures given; likewise, the deceptive cadence of the accompaniment to B flat at the close of the same—the voices, considered by themselves, making a cadence in D minor. This pedal point does not occur in the voices (1¼ measures excepted), but it is given to a part of the orchestral basses as well as to the organ. "Pedal point."

Such a pedal point may frequently *not* occur in the piano score, although it does in this instance. If it does in the orchestral basses, it should be reinforced by the organ as best qualified to sustain it.

It is evident, then, that the accompanist should familiarize himself in advance with the main features of the orchestral scoring of a given piece, especially as to the character and treatment of the basses. This applies particularly to such works as have not a definitely written out organ accompaniment by the composer.

Recurring to Example 167, we also observe that, in the second measure, the Soprano springs to the upper "A," and that the organ *does not* follow suit. The Sopranos are supported upon this high tone by the first Violins and two Oboes in unison. Supposing the accompaniment of this measure to have only a strong *eight-foot* registration, we see that the A of the accompaniment fills a gap in the vocal harmony between the Soprano and Alto. The fact is that sixteen-, four-, and two-foot stops are also employed here, the passage being *ff*. This gives the actual high A of the Sopranos, as well as the octave higher and lower; while the sense of a "filling-in" part, and of a blending together of the harmonies, is much better preserved by the form given. Were this vocal skip followed in the accompaniment, the organ would step into the foreground unduly through the octave repetition of its tone—eight, four, and two feet. High compass of Sopranos not followed by the Organ.

Attention is called to the progression of the Tenor, in the latter part of the second measure to the accent of the third, as compared with the same passage for the left hand in the accompaniment. It is seen that consecutive octaves are the result. Treatment of this kind should Purity of harmonic progression.

ordinarily be avoided.   The excuse here is that the vocal parts, considered by themselves, and the accompaniment, considered by itself, show two correct, though varied, leadings of the parts, with coincident harmonic progressions.   We give one more illustration, covering the sustaining of chords while voices move, as well as the avoidance of a high tone in the Soprano, from the first chorus of " Elijah," commencing with the 49th measure.

EXAMPLE 168.

The student should compare the above with the vocal score.

EXAMPLE 169.

Sustained tones with soft stops. Chromatic passing notes in Orchestra.

We cite Example 169, from Bach's " Passion Music, according to St. Matthew "* (No. 35), as an instance of sustained tones with soft stops.   The inexperienced organist or harmonist might well hesitate, in view of the passages given to the Flutes, to introduce sustained harmonies of this kind.   But a careful examination of the organ part, as compared with the melodic progression of the Flutes, will show that the majority of the tones belong to the essential harmony, and that the " passing notes " are comparatively few in number.   Of course, the registration must be so subordinated as in no way to cloud over or render doubtful the figuration in sixteenths.

* Piano score published by O. Ditson, Boston.

The student should observe the varied rhythmic support lent respectively by the stringed instruments and the two clarionets in unison. The strings will be but faintly heard here, but they will be *felt*.

Another example of the Orchestra preserving the rhythm.

It will also be seen that the organ part has been derived principally from the harmonies sustained by the Oboes and the stringed basses. The accompaniment, as originally written by Bach, comprised, beside the orchestral instruments, simply a "Continuo" (as described in the previous chapter), with the necessary thorough-bass figuration. The present "translation" of it into notes is from the celebrated score edition, edited by Robert Franz, and published by Breitkopf & Haertel, in Leipzig. In this, the obsolete wind instruments of Bach's day have been replaced by modern ones. The organ part has everywhere been written out in full, upon three staves, and in a most masterly way—in the very spirit of Bach himself—instead of depending upon the thorough-bass figuration. This great work is thus made available to modern conditions without losing any of its essentially original characteristics.

As soon as the student finds himself confronted with a work to which no special organ part has ever been written, but wherein, notwithstanding, the organ is expected to assume a prominent *rôle*; he must rely (in forming his accompaniment) upon the æsthetic significance of the piece, even more than upon the nature of the passages themselves, as being suited or not to the organ. Thus, at the beginning of the chorus, "For unto us a child is born," from Handel's "Messiah," the original organ part—if we may so term it—begins as follows:

Conditions to be observed when a work has no separate Organ Accompaniment.

EXAMPLE 170.

Organo e
Basso.

This is a "Continuo," and by no means very amply figured. The term "*Organo e Bassi*" (organ and orchestral basses) would imply that the organ should commence at once. This, however, is not traditional in this piece; for to begin at once is to throw away the subsequent climax. Besides this, the instrumentation of the opening is so thin, and the progression of the bass so marked, that the employment of the organ would here be positively injurious. The use of the pedal basses especially would tend to give a clumsy effect.

In this particular case, custom and common-sense have sanctioned reserving the organ until the first climax at the words, "Wonderful, Counsellor, the Mighty God," etc. After this, the organ may be sparingly employed, until the recurrence of the same passage in another key. After this, the organ part may again be continued to the close. So far as the "Continuo" may be accepted as indicating Handel's own intention, it was probably written for the harpsichord, which (as we have seen in a previous chapter) was then employed with the orchestra.

Reserving the Organ to heighten climaxes.

We have observed that the vocal parts, or at least their essential harmonies, constitute the player's guide in introducing the organ with orchestra. We now cite an instance, frequently occurring in Handel's music, where the voices have a continued florid figuration.

EXAMPLE 171.

For un - to us a child is born..........

un - to us   a Son is

giv - en,   un - to us   a Son   is giv - en.

Avoidance of florid figuration.

It is a virtual impossibility for voices, orchestra, and organ to move concisely together were the organ to play the florid voice parts of Example 171. This is not on account of any lack of capability in modern organs or executants, but rather on account of the distance of the organ from the voices and orchestra, as usually placed. Besides this, were it a perfectly feasible matter to get a united effect in such passages, it would deprive them of a certain lightness and fluency which must be their essential characteristic. The larger the chorus, the greater is this difficulty. This being the case, the organist turns to the essential harmonies, not considering the figuration except to avoid it, somewhat after the following manner:

EXAMPLE 172.

Cutting short of phrases. Use of the pedals only.

This example should be carefully compared with the preceding. It will be noticed how short the phrases are cut off in Example 172. This is absolutely necessary in order to preserve unity between orchestra, organ, and chorus. The same reason frequently leads to the use of the pedals only in florid accompaniments. This latter treatment can very frequently be adopted when the use of the manuals, in any form, would but tend to blur the effect desired.

Impossibility of relying upon the ear for unity of performance.

The organist who undertakes this class of accompaniment should be a perfectly steady and reliable "*timeist*," for nothing can more quickly disturb a chorus than to have the organist hold back the tempo. To the inexperienced player, it may seem a slight matter to avoid this fault. It is, on the contrary, extremely difficult. In case of a large chorus of four to six hundred voices, necessarily occupying considerable space, the collective tone always arrives perceptibly late to the ear of the accompanist. Should he strive to keep with the voices *as they sound to him*, the effect in the audience would be that of the accompaniment being constantly behind time.

Secondly, and in addition to this uncomfortable relation between voices and organ, the brass instruments and drums are generally placed at the rear, in close proximity to the organist, and between the chorus, the rest of the orchestra, and himself. These instruments (brass and drums) not only frequently prevent the organist from hearing the vocal parts, but their own part usually contains many syncopations or other deviations from the general rhythm. Meantime the sound of both voices and instruments is thrown out *from*, and not *towards*, the organist. *Other hindrances. The brass instruments and drums.*

Under such circumstances, the accompanist can depend but little upon his ear, but must rely almost exclusively upon the conductor; playing exactly with his beat. The difficulty is greatly enhanced by the fact that such precision on the part of the organist will (to *his* ear) *seemingly* produce an *anticipation* of given harmonies; as though the organ were in advance of the rest of the instrumental and choral forces. None who have not had actual experience with a large chorus can imagine how difficult it is, at first, not to yield in tempo. Only in this way, however, can true precision, which will be recognized by the audience as such, be attained.

When the number of performers is very large, the organist should all but anticipate the conductor's beat.

The same precision is requisite at the close of phrases where the organ ceases and the orchestra continues. This is especially necessary at the final close of a piece. Here the slightest "after-sound" of the organ is very offensive when orchestra and voices cease promptly. The player must remove both hands and feet from the instrument simultaneously with the sign from the conductor. Nor is it allowable for the pedal tone to linger a moment, as we have seen is frequently done with good effect, in church music, the organ being then the only accompanying instrument. That Mendelssohn realized the importance of this cessation of tone may be seen by comparing the close of Example 104 with the voice parts. (See piano score of "Elijah.") *Avoidance of "after-tone" at final close.*

We now proceed to give certain extracts from the organ accompaniment to Mendelssohn's "Elijah." The student should carefully compare them with the piano score at least, viewing the piano score as an outline of the orchestral accompaniment. *Examples for comparison from "Elijah."*

EXAMPLE 173.

In this example, it is evident that the pedal should be used in the lower octave during the *ff*. Neither is it necessary to repeat the chords, as given in the first four measures, in view of the accentuation of the voices and the figuration of the orchestral accompaniment. Beginning with the ninth measure, the pedal only is employed.

Manner of Study. The student will find it a great source of improvement if, in such cases as the above, he ask himself, "*Why* has the author done this?" Careful study of voice parts, accompaniment, and organ part will almost invariably reveal the reason.

EXAMPLE 174.

EXAMPLE 175.

EXAMPLE 176.

EXAMPLE 177.

Observe in Examples 176 and 177 the relations of the accompaniment as given to voices and orchestra.

In leaving the student to pursue this study at his own option, it is simply necessary to call attention to one or two points, by way of summing up the requirements of this class of accompaniment. Musicianship required.

(1.) In employing the organ with orchestra, it is musicianship rather than mere technique that is required, although the technique must be ample.

(2.) The organist must have nerve to follow the conductor steadily. He must do this regardless of conflicting sounds arising from acoustic relations, and produced by the grouping of a large number of vocal and instrumental performers. Nerve.

(3.) He must so handle his instrument, that, except in the rarest instances, it does not obtrude its tone upon the ear, but blends into the general tone mass. It is manifest that the more familiar he may be with the nature and construction of an orchestral score, the more readily he can solve the problem presented to him. In this connection, it would prove exceedingly profitable for the student to possess himself of the complete organ part to "Elijah" and the "Hymn of Praise." The full score of Bach's "Passion Music," also his "Magnificat" (both edited by Franz), containing the organ accompaniment in full upon three staves, offer most extended and valuable material for further study of this subject. Familiarity with the work to be performed.

CONCLUDING REMARKS.

Résumé.

In the preceding pages, it has been the author's endeavor to make clear some of the modes of treating the organ as an accompanying instrument.

He has striven to show that, while the pianist may confine himself to the notes of an accompaniment as he finds them, the organist must modify the same in many cases, in order to adapt them to his instrument.

If this has been understood, it must have been perceived that such deviations from the exact notation have not been idly made, but were advocated for the purpose of conforming to the spirit, rather than to the letter, of a given composition; also to afford the voices unimpeded support.

He has further endeavored to make evident that an accompaniment must not be considered by itself, but in its compound relation to the voice or voices accompanied; the two elements together forming the complete whole.

Rehearsal with Piano instead of Organ.

Although no better support for voices can be found than that afforded by the organ, it nevertheless frequently proves a poor instrument *to rehearse with.* Both its merits and defects as an instrument contribute to this result.

In the first place, the distinctness with which it sustains every tone of the harmony, causes it to render *too much* support to the voices for purposes of rehearsal. Besides this, it measurably prevents the organist (supposing him to be the director of the choir, which he always should be) from accurately hearing the mistakes and faults of the singers, especially if the choir is a large one.

In securing promptness of accentuation and rhythm, in the first practice of a new composition, the piano is far preferable to the organ.

When a choir has once made itself fairly familiar with a piece, the organ will then furnish all the rhythmic accent necessary, if properly handled. The piano, beyond securing intonation and accent, does not support the voices in the sense that the organ accomplishes this. With the piano, the singers are forced to rely upon themselves to a far greater extent, and defects in performance are far more readily detected.

For these reasons, every choir should hold their rehearsals, of new compositions at least, with piano. Afterwards the piece may be rehearsed with the organ, if, in the judgment of the director, it is necessary. This will sometimes be the case, more especially in pieces provided with an obligato accompaniment for the organ.

Rehearsal without Accompaniment.

The young organist taking charge of a choir will likewise find the frequent rehearsal *without accompaniment* (or such portions of pieces as seem to present peculiar difficulties) to be of the greatest value. In this way, even timid singers learn to be independent, while the director can give his entire attention to the true balance of the voices. This is the more important, as even in choirs (quartet or chorus) where the parts may be termed well balanced, it is frequently necessary for one part to sing louder or softer than another. This occurs not merely in case of a melodic design, which is intended to be "brought out" in some particular part; it may also be necessary to the proper blending of a single chord. Here it becomes the director's duty to see that the voices which have such intervals as fourths and fifths do not unduly assert themselves, and that the thirds and sixths are so sustained that the harmony may seem complete to the ear.

Glancing back over the various chapters of this work, the author is fully sensible of many shortcomings in the presentation of the different subjects. He has been encouraged to proceed, however, by the fact that no previous attempt has been made (so far as he is aware) to put in print a certain amount of what may be termed "traditional matter" bearing upon accompaniment. The various organ "methods" have but little or nothing to say on this subject, nor does it strictly come within their province. Our better organists become familiar with various modes and expedients in organ accompaniment, partly from some good teacher's example, and partly through their own natural talent. In the latter case, such knowledge comes to them after long experience, and as a result of familiarity with the nature of voices, as well as with that of their instrument.

It furthermore comes to them in the light of an original discovery in this direction.

To hasten such discoveries has been the principal purpose of the preceding pages.

It may possibly seem discouraging to some readers of this work that they are called upon to familiarize themselves with *so many* points of treatment, often trifling in themselves, in order to accompany well.

To such faint-hearted ones, the author would fain say a word or two in conclusion.

He has not pretended to treat his subject exhaustively, and therefore fully believes that any church-player (to be thoroughly worthy of the name of a good choir-accompanist) must be familiar with the majority of the ideas herein advanced; even if he apply the principles they involve in a practically unconscious manner.

As regards counsel and advice towards accomplishing this end, no language of his own could here prove so applicable as the following golden lines of encouragement :

> "The more an artist faithful toils,
> The more unto his work gives heed,
> So much the more doth he succeed.
> Therefore each day thy task renew,
> And thou shalt see what *that* will do ;
> Thereby each purpose is attained,
> Thereby what seemed so hard is gained,
> And, step by step, thou shalt discern
> The knowledge which thy hand must learn."
>
> GOETHE (" *Artists' Apotheosis*").

FINIS.

INDEX.